SLACKS AND CALLUSES

Slacks and Calluses

Our Summer in a Bomber Factory

CONSTANCE BOWMAN REID

Illustrated by CLARA MARIE ALLEN

Introduction by SANDRA M. GILBERT

SMITHSONIAN BOOKS

Washington

Library of Congress Cataloging-in-Publication Data

Reid, Constance.

[Slacks and callouses]

Slacks and calluses : our summer in a bomber factory / Constance Bowman ;
illustrated by Clara Marie Allen ; introduction by Sandra M. Gilbert.

    p.   cm.

Originally published: Slacks and callouses. 1st ed. New York : Toronto :
Longmans, Green & Co., 1944.

ISBN 1-56098-368-X (alk. paper)

    1. B-24 bomber—Design and construction Anecdotes.   2. Women aircraft
industry workers—United States Anecdotes.   3. United States—Social
life and customs Anecdotes.   4. World War, 1939–1945—United States
Anecdotes.   5. Reid, Constance Anecdotes.   6. Allen, Clara Marie Anecdotes.
I. Title.

TL724.R45   1999

940.53′73′0922—dc21   99-31365
                                                                        CIP

British Library Cataloguing-in-Publication Data available

Manufactured in the United States of America
06 05 04   6 5 4 3

  ∞ ✪   The recycled paper used in this publication meets the minimum
requirements of the American National Standard for Information Sciences—
Permanence of Paper for Printed Library Materials ANSI Z39.48-1984.

CONTENTS

INTRODUCTION
"Was That a Liberator?"
Sandra M. Gilbert

The time: 1943.

The place: Sunny San Diego, bustling with naval bases and aircraft factories, where two feisty young women have decided to do their bit for the War Effort by spending their two-month summer vacation building bombers.

The heroines: writer Constance Bowman, a high school journalism and English teacher, and her friend, illustrator Clara Marie Allen, a high school art teacher.

The true story, "as true as we could make it" [vii]: a figuratively riveting account of the literal riveting as well as the other workday events that ensued when, as Bowman explains, even after "people *laughed* when we announced that the aircraft industry wanted *us* to build bombers during summer vacation," the two friends went to work because "Clara Marie said by golly, she could build bombers and I said by golly, I could too, although I wasn't quite sure what either of us could do to bombers—that would be useful" [1].

And for those who've forgotten just what life on the Home Front was like way back then or those who want to refresh their memories—along with the myriad boomers and Generation X-ers too young to remember such a time—this memoir will be an

NOTE: Numbers in brackets indicate page references to the text. The use of italics—about which see p. 181—is faithful to the text.

engrossing read, starting with the book title's evocation of both costume and labor.

Slacks! In an era when even great-grandmothers cheerfully don stylish pantsuits in preparation for a night at the opera, it may be as hard for alumnae of the forties as it is for with-it teenagers to grasp the enormous change in lifestyle implied by the very idea of women in trousers. To be sure, women began to change their customary costume as far back as the eighteen fifties, when Amelia Bloomer pioneered the culotte-like pantaloons that bear her name to this day. But arguably the first key moment of metamorphosis in female dress came during World War I when women war workers confronted the same needs for practical on-the-job clothing that women like Bowman and Allen faced during World War II. At that point women in England's "Land Army" together with factory "girls" on both sides of the Atlantic took up breeches and overalls, jumpsuits and jodhpurs, in enthusiastic numbers. By the thirties, slacks (and shorts and "evening pajamas") were certainly acceptable leisure wear for well-bred women but, as Bowman shows, the appearance of such garments in the workplace and on the street had powerful class implications.

Incisively yet good-humoredly focused on what might be called the "theory and practice of the wearing of slacks," chapter nine of the Bowman and Allen saga is a small gem of social history. "It was bad enough being tired all the time and dirty most of the time, but worst of all the first week was having to go to work in slacks," Bowman declares, noting that on such occasions "people who knew us acted as if they didn't" while "people who didn't know us whistled as if they did," for in "war-time San Diego there are just two kinds of women: the ones who go to work in skirts and the ones who go in slacks," with the former considered far the more respectable. Indeed, observes the author, though the "girls who work in slacks are sometimes cleaner and neater than the girls who work in skirts" and though they "usually make more money than their skirted sisters," they are treated with condescension because "they are women who work in slacks instead of skirts"—and if "you don't think there's a difference, just put on a Consolidated [aircraft factory] uniform and try to get service in your favorite store, make a reservation at a ticket office, or get information at the post office" [67].

Bowman's analysis of the problem is subtle and persuasive, though it will probably surprise readers at this end of the twentieth century, for she argues that even while the wearing of slacks *de*feminized women factory workers, paradoxically it also eroticized them, making them seem more sexually available because less genteel. Her discussion of this conundrum is worth attention:

> It was bad enough to have clerks ignore us, to have the members of our own sex scorn us, but what really hurt was the attitude of men. In one way, we were not women at all as far as they were concerned—if having them give us their seats on a crowded bus or stand aside to let us pass or pick up something we dropped meant that we were women. In another way, we were definitely women to them—"skirts" is the old-fashioned term, although it isn't appropriate today. Men lounging on corners looked us over in a way we didn't like. . . . Men grabbed us and followed us and whistled at us. They called us "Sister" in a most unbrotherly way and "Baby" in a most unfatherly way. [69]

Bowman doesn't brood excessively on the class implications of this situation, but she does quite frankly confess that she and her buddy Clara Marie find it what we now call consciousness raising:

> It was a great shock to C.M. and me to find that being a lady depended more upon our clothes than upon ourselves. We had always gone on the theory that the only girls men tried to pick up were the ones who looked as if they could be picked up. Armed in our dignified school-teacherhood and our glasses, we were content to go unmolested with only a reas-

suring whistle now and then from a truck driver or a soldier in a jeep. This summer we found out that it was not our innate dignity that protected us from unwelcome attentions, but our trim suits, big hats, white gloves, and spectator pumps. Clothes, we reflected sadly, make the woman—and some clothes make the man think that he can make the woman. [69]

There is, of course, a comically pedagogical tone to that last sentence, but for the most part, school-teacher though she is, Bowman refrains from lecturing on the multiple class and gender hierarchies she and C.M. encounter as they penetrate further into the heretofore unknown realm of slacks and calluses. Rather, her narrative dramatizes these hierarchies in a number of other ways. Hair, for instance, constitutes an ongoing problem for the women who build the big bombers.

"I do not allow girls to work without hair coverings," announces the pompous foreman of our heroines' unit (who himself is defined by a uniform that makes him look "like a little boy, mainly because the sleeves of his blue shirt were cut off above the elbow"), and though Bowman and C.M. decide that "Mr. B.'s bark had no bite" after they notice that most female workers ("nine out of fourteen") are laboring "*without* hair coverings" [24, 25], a major crisis strikes when weeks later all the "girls" are ordered to cover their hair with caps or risk dismissal. Both the absurdity of the order and its implicit misogyny are revealed by "Miller, a mannish-looking woman with a boyish bob" when she comments that "I asked Billings why I have to wear a cap when my hair is *shorter* than his, and he said that even if I shaved it all off, I'd have to wear a cap" [157]. But Bowman's concise summary of the workers' priorities ("any woman could understand why with a choice between beauty and safety, she would take beauty") is as telling as the exuberant, quasi-feminist insurrection that leads to the fore*men's* realization that "it was impossible (1) to get the girls in caps, (2) to keep them in caps, (3) to make them put their hair under the caps—unless the foremen were willing to devote all of their time to achieve these three things" [163].

For if the wearing of slacks makes women "not women at all" in one way and "definitely women" in another way, the battle of the sexes that the factory "girls" wage over hairstyle exposes gender ambiguities that contemporary feminists will understand very well. On the one hand, in choosing beauty over safety the workers are obviously collaborating in just the eroticization of the woman-in-slacks about which Bowman and C.M. protest when they complain about "clothes [that] make the man think that he can make the woman" [69]. On the other hand, in refusing to wear the drab regulation caps that would deprive them of their individuality as well as their personal freedom to choose, the "girls" are declining to join the masculine realm of regulations and uniforms ruled by the bureaucratically inclined foremen, affirming instead a more joyous and mischievous regimen of feminine misrule. By the time the battle ends, Bowman tells us, her colleagues are sporting a hilarious range of caps and hairstyles ("enormous fuzzy knitted turbans," a bandana that leaves a "magnificent blond pompadour . . . uncovered," a regulation cap turned backward "like a tam," a "triangular felt peasant cap that had a gay bunch of felt flowers attached to each side") and, significantly, the "*only* woman wearing a cap that covered *all* her hair was the Women's Counselor, who was trying to be an *example*" [163].

But of course the women who work at Consolidated aren't just "girls" because they are women, they're "girls" because they're working-class women, and perhaps it is their temporary sojourn in the working class that teaches our two young teacher-heroines the most. To be sure, Bowman and C.M. are never in the least snobbish; they deplore male refusals to surrender bus seats to even the sexiest "Baby" or "Sister" in slacks. Yet Bowman quite astutely inspects her own deep professional (and thus middle-class) identification when one of the foremen asks her to teach a newcomer how to install safety belt holders:

> All of a sudden I was a teacher, not an aircraft worker. . . . I noticed the change in the way I stood, the way I answered Mr. MacGregor, and the way I appraised "Miss Martin." I think I felt the way Mr. Hyde must have felt when he suddenly turned back into Dr. Jekyll [109].

As both a writer and an English teacher, moreover, Bowman takes a kind of clinical interest in some of her coworkers' odder usages—"Vacational School" for Vocational School [43], or "unconnect" for disconnect [112]. Ultimately both she and C.M. respond to such usages, however, as well as to the droll remarks they record, with affectionate pleasure. Bowman agrees with one worker, for instance, that "putting in pipes is awfully hard on your religion" [94] and is intrigued by the observation of another that "I'm allergic to electricity. . . . It runs in my family. My uncle was electrocuted." (Her own reply—"That must have been quite a shock"—is equally memorable. [50])

Bowman's evident fondness for her colleagues infuses her often moving portraits of the diverse women-in-slacks who labor nightly building bombers on the Swing Shift. In the course of *Slacks and Calluses* we meet a range of workers, many of whom wistfully confess that, as one puts it, "I'd like to have my high school diploma" [112]. Bowman introduces us to "Emeline, [who] had not finished school because there had not been enough children for a high school in the thinly populated section of New Mexico where she lived" [112]; to "Mary, a tiny girl [who] had had to leave school in the ninth grade when her father died, leaving her mother with half a dozen younger boys and girls to support" [112]; to "Nancy, [the] ridiculously young" mother of two who "had left school to get married" [113]; to "Mattie [who] had dropped out of school in the tenth grade because her step-father had felt that a girl of sixteen should be earning her own living" [113]; and to a number of other women whose personal histories help expand our sense of the public history in which all are caught up. At the same time, Bowman also draws shrewd, sometimes sympathetic and sometimes sardonic, pictures of the male supervisors (otherwise known as "Red Buttons" or "foremens" [*sic*]) who try—occasionally in vain—to rule the lives of these now and then unruly "girls." Among these men is the big boss, one "Cuthbert J. Plunkett," about whom she wickedly remarks that "we always expected a sudden darkening over the line and a rustle of wings as Mr. Plunkett passed by" [117].

Clearly the foremen and the workers aren't always on the best of terms. With the exception of the punctiliously polite and teacherly Bowman and C.M., who always refer to and address the Red Buttons as "Mister," all the other workers refuse on principle "to Mister [anybody], especially a Damn Red Button" [117]. But both workers and foremen are drawn together by the arduousness and often the urgency of the tasks they have in common. Bowman and C.M. are commendably insouciant and irreverent; much of the time they're unsentimental about the terrible exigencies of the war that brought them onto the production line at Consolidated in the first place. They're as amused as they're bemused by tool boxes and time clocks, as comic about the procedures "on the line" as they are awed by the big bombers out "on the field." But the calluses they earn from their labor are as crucial to their story as the slacks they have to learn to wear on the job. Here's Bowman on what it meant to install safety belt holders on B-24s, the task she's given her first night at work:

> For every holder I had installed, I had squatted, kneeled, bent, and sat on the floor. I had gritted my teeth, clutched my motor, and pushed as hard as I could push. I had stubbed my toes, cracked my shins, and knocked my head three times on the metal sill above the safety belt holders. I had broken my fingernails, I had cut my fingers, and once I had almost bitten

through my tongue, which in moments of stress I stick out and curl around my right cheek. [42]

And C.M., assigned to a job in the cramped bomb bay, testifies that the "Black Hole of Calcutta was *nothing* compared to the Black Hole of Bomb Bay" [90]. "That was the Swing Shift for you!" the two declare. "Sleep. Eat. Work. Wash. Sleep. Eat. Work. Wash"—even though, with characteristic good humor, they insist all the exercise has been so beneficial that a friend told them they "must be having a wonderful time" on their summer vacation [66].

But despite its comic élan, its tough-minded refusal of easy sentimentality, *Slacks and Calluses* is a patriotic book. How could it not be, considering the emergencies of the era in which it was written? Its unembarrassed patriotism, like the old-fashioned courtesy with which Mr. Billings, the unit foreman, introduces the newly hired Bowman and C.M. to their supervisors ("Mrs. Allen, Mr. Tompkinson," he said. "Mr. Tompkinson will be your leadman, Mrs. Allen. And Miss Bowman and Miss Leroy, Mr. MacGregor" [25]) may now seem strange to cynical readers brought up to mistrust the past's communal imperatives. Yet Bowman brings both private and public history to life with such vivacity that, despite our "postmodern" irony, we're moved when the otherwise obnoxious Billings confesses "in the embarrassed gruff manner of a football coach before the big game" that he wants to "get the ships to fly" because the "important thing is that I have two brothers out there, flying these ships" [25]. And doubters though many of us may be, we empathize with Bowman and C.M. when they eat their "sandwiches outside by the field where we could watch the finished Liberators warm up" because "from the first, we looked at them critically and proudly, much as a mother would look at her children" [55]. If "the dollars that we made were few, the bombers that we built were many," the memoirist confesses in her last chapter, noting that "after a summer on the production line we looked at a Liberator the way you gaze in awe at a great tapestry when the note under it says that it took a hundred women twenty years to make it" because "Liberators are just that hand-made" [174].

"We looked at them critically and proudly": given the hindsight afforded by precisely the postmodern perspective that may make Bowman's and Allen's patriotic stance seem dubious to some end-of-the-century observers, that phrase takes on special resonance. Writing in 1943, Bowman reports with excitement on a "recent innovation" in the B-24 called the belly gun turret that "we were informed was worth five thousand dollars all by itself" and "was always a favorite of mine, for it had the round placid look of Tik Tok of Oz" [78]. She couldn't have known—though no doubt she later found out—how dreadful a place that turret, in the words of the poet Randall Jarrell, was for the "one man, a short small man" assigned to it:

> When this gunner tracked with his machine guns a fighter attacking his bomber from below, he revolved with the turret; hunched upside-down in his little sphere, he looked like the foetus in the womb. The fighters which attacked him were armed with cannon firing explosive shells.*

About this turret gunner Jarrell in 1945 published perhaps the single most concisely powerful poem of the war, a five-line verse entitled *The Death of the Ball Turret Gunner* relating the fate of one such "hunched upside-down" soldier, who "woke to black flak and the nightmare fighters":

> When I died they washed me out of the turret with a hose.

The hose, explained Jarrell, as anxious for accuracy as Bowman, "was a steam hose."

---

* On the air war and the Jarrell poem, see Sandra M. Gilbert and Susan Gubar, *No Man's Land: The Place of the Woman Writer in the Twentieth Century*, vol. 3: *Letters from the Home Front* (New Haven: Yale University Press, 1994), ch. 5, "Charred Skirts and Deathmask: World War II and the Blitz on Women," pp. 211–65, especially 214–15.

"History," wrote T. S. Eliot in *Gerontion*, "has many cunning passages" and elicits "supple confusions," another way of saying that certain ironies are inevitably part of the aftermath rather than functions of the present. Bowman and C.M. aren't wrong in their enthusiasm and pride, even if at times the Liberators whose design they believed they'd helped improve ultimately ended up entrapping, rather than freeing, some of the very men for whom they were trying to "get the ships to fly." As for the Home Front: did the Liberators liberate the authors of *Slacks and Calluses*—and their sister workers—from a world in which women were "girls" and men were "Misters"? Films like *Rosie the Riveter* suggest that female laborers were "put [back] in their places" when the war was over, another problem neither of these enterprising young women could have anticipated, and certainly the ideology of the fifties was so determinedly antifeminist that formerly trouser-clad war workers were often happy to don the girdles, petticoats, and long full skirts of the old-fashioned "New Look."

But women like Bowman and C.M. couldn't be "put in their places" on the Home Front that easily—and their book clearly isn't about retreat. On the contrary, it's a chapter in the ongoing history of a momentous advance, a tale of two women, along with thousands like them, who infiltrated a male-dominated realm of time clocks, welding torches, tool cribs, and bomb bays, heralding all the feminist forays into the public sphere that were to mark the second half of our century. With its vivid evocations of life on the production line and its high-spirited drawings, *Slacks and Calluses* endures as lively testimony to the sometimes painful ambiguities, the often poignant drama, and even, at times, the curiously genial comedy of what Bowman defines as "the minutes that made the man-hours that built the bombers that would bomb Berlin and Tokyo"[55]. The man-hours and, as we've seen, the woman-hours.

PREFACE (1944)

This is a true story, as true as we could make it, because we want to show you what a bomber production line is really like. It isn't an exciting story — except that helping to build the bombers that are leading the invasion *is* exciting — but it is an exact story. We are school teachers. We did spend our summer vacation on the Consolidated swing shift. We did work in Department 192, "out of" Station 20. But if you should go to Department 192, you would not find Mr. Billings or Mr. MacGregor or any of the other people we have written about (except Mr. Ely, who has been kind enough to give us permission to use his name). You would find, however, a great many foremen who are like Mr. Billings, because he is like all foremen, just as Mr. MacGregor is like all leadmen. You would even find people who are like us — because we are like all the thousands of school teachers who have spent their summer vacations "Keeping 'Em Flying."

CONSTANCE BOWMAN
CLARA MARIE ALLEN

July 1944
San Diego, California

CHAPTER ONE

ANYBODY can build bombers—if we could.

We were the kind of girls who knew nothing about airplanes except that they had wings and they flew. When one flew overhead we waited until somebody said, "That's a Liberator!" Then we looked into the sky and echoed wisely, "Yes, it is, isn't it?" We were not sure then whether a Liberator was an army or a navy plane, or whether it was a bomber or a fighter; and we had not yet discovered that a B-24 and a Liberator are exactly the same thing.

Perhaps that was why people *laughed* when we announced that the aircraft industry wanted *us* to build bombers during summer vacation. Perhaps that was why they rolled on the floor and shrieked.

"*You* build bombers!" they howled. "An *art* teacher and an *English* teacher!"

That was the way they said it, laughing uproariously — just as if an art teacher and an English teacher *couldn't* build bombers. That was enough for us. Clara Marie said by golly, she could build bombers and I said by golly, I could too, although I wasn't quite sure what either of us could do to bombers—that would be useful. Anyhow *that* was the aircraft industry's problem. They needed help. They wanted school teachers to work during summer vacation. O.K., they had to find something school teachers like us could do.

At least we let the aircraft industry know what they

were up against, for we filled out our applications for employment with perfect honesty — putting "No" or "None" after *every* question. Then, a little embarrassed at our own effrontery in thinking we could be of any use on the production line, we took our applications down to the Employment Office. We maneuvered our swooping hats into position before a tiny window which was presided over by a clerk whose name, according to the little metal standard at her elbow, appropriately was Mrs. Hires. We deposited our applications timidly in front of her.

Mrs. Hires, to our amazement, greeted our applications with expressions of joy. She didn't even look at the "No's" and the "None's." She didn't seem the least bit worried about what we could do on the production line. She just wanted to be sure that we understood ours would not be *clean* jobs. She asked twice did we understand that we would get our hands *dirty*. As soon as we had assured her that we understood—we were hired!

"What shift do you want to work?" she asked.

"What shifts do you have?" parried C.M., who is like that, while I said quickly, "The Swing Shift." (The Swing Shift pay-rate, which is eight cents more an hour than the Day Shift, was a useful item of information I had gleaned from a theme on "My Job" in my first period English class, the theme explaining incidentally why the writer usually slept through first period English, if he got there at all, which he usually didn't.)

"Which plant?" Mrs. Hires asked patiently, explaining that the Swing Shift at the Main Plant was from 4:30 to 1 and the one at the Parts Plant from 2:30 to 11.

C.M. looked at me, and I looked at her, and we both did some rapid figuring about getting up and going to bed and getting our summer tans on the beach.

"4:30 to 1," said C.M.

"4:30 to 1," I said.

2

Mrs. Hires looked *pleased.* She said that people were *needed* on that shift.

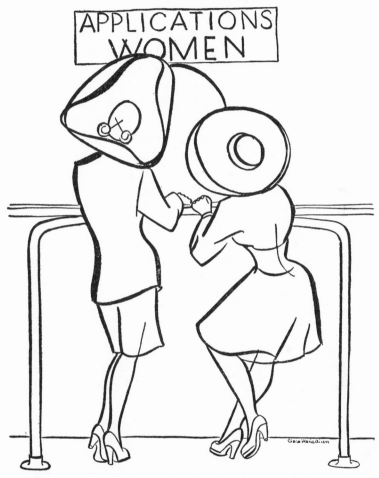

We maneuvered our swooping hats into position . . .

"Now *what* do you want to do?" she asked, and the way she asked it sounded as if she meant what could we do.

"What *can* we do?" we echoed plaintively.

Mrs. Hires opened an official-looking folder.

"Well," she said, as if it were not too difficult a problem, "filing," (filing metal, not cards, she hastened to explain), "riveting, sub-assembly, final installations—"

"*Final* installations?" we demanded, snatching at the word *Final*. "Actually in the plane?"

"Yes, actually in the plane," she said.

"Are you *sure*," I said cautiously, for after all we were patriotic Americans, "are you sure that we *can* make final installations?"

"Oh, of course, anybody can," she said carelessly, and she made strange little marks on our applications and wrote our names in the spaces marked "Last Name First" and sternly stamped in red "Applicant Will Not Write His Own Name Here."

"Now this will expedite matters for you," she told us. "You will report here Monday morning at 8 o'clock, and I will have your applications checked by then. That will *expedite* your Employment Induction," she pointed out sweetly.

Expedite, she said. That was undoubtedly the favorite word of the aircraft industry; and if at the time we thought that the aircraft industry didn't know what it meant, that was before we had been "expedited" through the conveyor-belt process known as Employment Induction.

Our Employment Induction *began* at 8 o'clock Monday morning when we graciously announced to Mrs. Hires that we were now ready to build bombers, and it *ended* at 10 o'clock when we and our personalities had been reduced to half a hundred forms, cards, folders, and contracts, all signed in duplicate "where the check is, please."

First, Mrs. Hires gave each of us a bulging 9 by 11 manila envelope which contained seven handbooks and pamphlets, a list of regulations for women's work clothes, a list of the tools we would need, a copy of *The Consolidated News,* and a membership card for the aircraft union. She said she *thought* the envelope contained all the information we would need. We thought that it must.

"Do you have any questions?" she asked. She knew that we didn't, because she had just said that *all* the information we would need was in the envelope; but evidently she liked to prove to herself the super-efficiency of the Employment Induction: Every question answered before it was asked.

"Just follow the instructions on the envelope — and follow the yellow line on the floor," she told us.

We followed the yellow line around the corner and into a large office where there were at least three dozen desks, each complete with typewriter and typist. C.M. and I took our places on the row of chairs along the wall and inspected the other new employees who were there ahead of us. They were evidently the scrapings from the manpower barrel — like us. Older women and old men. Scrawny mothers with children tugging at the hems of their housedresses. Fuzzy high school boys.

There were nine steps listed in the procedure for Employment Induction, which was mimeographed on the front of our envelopes; and there were about that many physical steps, since we usually moved from chair to chair and desk to desk as different girls, all spreading at the hips, all wearing glasses, all glancing worriedly at the sheets in their typewriters, called "Bowman!" or "Allen!," never looking up to see who Bowman or Allen was as we handed over our envelopes. This way we moved down the yellow line, the envelopes growing bulkier at each step.

Step one.

The Requisition Clerk entered on a permanent record our names (now officially C.M. Allen and C.H. Bowman), our job classification (*un*classified and *un*skilled), our starting date (Wednesday afternoon at 4:30), and our rate of pay (60 cents an hour with an 8 cent bonus for the Swing Shift).

"Do you have any questions?" she asked, stuffing more bright colored sheets of paper into our envelopes.

We didn't.

Step two.

The Physical Appointment Clerk filled in a description of each of us on half a dozen assorted identification cards. She looked disapprovingly at C.M.'s personal description as it was checked in on her application. Then she looked at C.M.'s eyes.

"I'm sorry," she said, "but we will have to change the color of your eyes. We don't have green eyes here.

"Do you have any questions?" she asked absent-mindedly as she crossed out "green" and wrote "hazel" after "Color of Eyes."

We didn't.

Step three.

The Birth Certificate Clerk was having her troubles as we arrived.

"I wired for my birth certificate," wailed the girl in front of us, "but they just wired back a list of lawyers who can start proceedings to prove that I was born!"

The Birth Certificate Clerk took our birth certificates and scrutinized them carefully. She seemed to be satisfied that we had been born.

"Do you have any questions?" she asked as she returned them to us.

We didn't.

Step four.

The Clock Clerk gave us each a number (4126 for C.M. and 4042 for me) and said sternly that we should read the instructions which we would find in our envelopes on punching in and out at the time clock. We had already read the instructions, which had sub-points lettered from "A" to "J," and we were already convinced that we were utterly incapable of coping with a complex machine like a time clock.

"Do you have any questions?" the Clock Clerk said, quickly handing back our envelopes so that we wouldn't ask any.

We didn't.

Step five.

The Identification Clerk filled out a stack of cards for each of us and then shoved them across the desk for our signatures.

"Do you have any questions?" she asked as C.M. scrawled her name and I laboriously drew mine so that it would be legible.

We didn't.

Step six.

The War Manpower Commission Availability Certificate Clerk (whew!) asked us if we had Availability Certificates. When we admitted that we didn't, she said well, she didn't think we needed them anyway.

"You *are* available," she said, as if it were the only thing she could find in our favor.

"That's us," said C.M. cheerfully. "We are available."

"Do you have any questions?" asked the clerk, ignoring this small pleasantry.

We didn't.

Step seven.

The Fingerprint Clerk greeted us briskly.

"Put your purse here," he said to me as we came in. "Put your glasses there. Get in here. Stand there. Look here." He held a card up under my chin. I didn't know whether it was a name or a number, but I smiled my most bewitching smile, which looked like a leer when I saw it later on my identification photo. Since my smile had obviously been a failure, C.M. tried an expression of haughty interest when it was her turn. It also looked like a leer on the finished photo.

"Re-lax!" the clerk instructed me, taking my right hand firmly in his as if it didn't belong to me at all. He rolled my thumb on the ink pad and then on the card with a rocking motion like that of a waltz — if a waltz had two dips instead of one. While my hand was practically waltzing without me, I tried to follow with the rest of my body. I had the embarrassed feeling I have when I step on my partner's toes. C.M. watched me carefully so that she would do better, which she did.

"Do you have any questions?" asked the Fingerprint Clerk as he studied my left thumbprint critically. He was obviously a *master* who had fingerprinted gangster kings and stock exchange presidents.

We didn't.

Step eight.

The Physical Examination Clerk, efficiently clattering on her keyboard, typed out our medical folders without an error. The nurse, letter perfect, rattled off a list of peculiarly uncheerful ailments in double time.

"Did you ever have rheumatism? Kidney trouble? Typhoid? Small pox? Syphilis? Cancer? Varicose veins?"

We said, "No. No. No." Sometimes we stuck in an extra "No" and sometimes we got behind and missed one. Once we said "No" from force of habit when we should have said "Yes."

The second nurse, efficient as always, snatched us up as we said the last "No" and assigned us to barren little individual dressing rooms. A few minutes later a third nurse called "Bowman!" and "Allen!," and the rest of the physical examination was like any other — poke, push, probe, and punch.

The blonde girl in front of me, whose mother hovered over her even in the doctor's office, was illiterate, as the nurse discovered when she tried to give her an eye test. The nurse told us that she was the first illiterate in nearly a thousand women, although the rate among the men hired was higher. C.M. said she supposed that illiterate men had to get jobs while illiterate women had children. The nurse said that she supposed so, and deposited us again in the little dressing rooms.

"Do you have any questions?" she called after us a few minutes later as we followed the yellow line back into the Employment Office.

We didn't.

Step nine.

The Final Induction Clerk, calling "Bowman!" and "Allen!" for the last time, put a sheaf of papers in front of us for us to sign, most of which involved reducing our pay checks by bond, tax, and insurance deductions. I unsuccessfully tried to subtract all these from 68 cents times 52 hours, which I was multiplying in my head. Some of the papers were in very fine print, which we conscientiously tried to read before we signed them. One was an Invention Agreement "entered into by and between Consolidated Vultee Aircraft (hereinafter called the Company) and Constance Hall Bowman and Clara Marie Allen (hereinafter called the Employees). Witnesseth: in consideration of the mutual undertakings hereinafter set forth, the parties hereto do hereby agree as follows:" the general idea being that if we built better mousetraps, Consolidated could keep the world from our door. We thought that it was very flattering of Consolidated to be so interested in our inventions, although we could have told them they wouldn't be worth the trouble.

We also signed a sheet saying that we had read the Espionage Act, Executive Order of the President of the

United States, No. 8381, and that we had been warned that many of the projects carried on by ·the company were classified as *Secret, Confidential,* and *Restricted.* C.M. asked the Final Induction Clerk how we would know whether a project was Secret, Confidential, or merely Restricted. The clerk merely smiled wisely and said, "You'll know."

"Probably the guard will say 'Shhh!' when we go in," I whispered to C.M.

"Now," said the Final Induction Clerk with a sigh as she wrote down on our envelopes the same instructions she was giving us, "you will report to Gate Two, Plant One, at 4:30 on Wednesday afternoon. Wednesday afternoon," she repeated. "You will be unclassified helpers, final minor installations on the B-24's."

"On the *big bombers?*" we asked.

The Final Induction Clerk smiled kindly and said yes, on the *big bombers.*

"Do you have any questions?" she asked, confidently, because she knew we couldn't possibly have any. It was the final test of the efficiency of the Employment Induction.

We said no, we didn't have any questions. If we had had the strength to think of any, we wouldn't have had the strength to ask them. We felt as weak as triplicate copies of ourselves. As we staggered out into the morning sunshine, C.M. cast a thoughtful if slightly jaundiced eye at the Army and Navy "E" flying on its own standard next to the American flag over the main entrance of the plant.

"The Army and Navy 'E'," she mused. "I bet the 'E' stands for *expedite!*"

CHAPTER TWO

T*HE BIG BOMBERS!*
Every time we said it, they got *bigger* and we got smaller
until by 4:30 Wednesday afternoon C.M. was saying ac-
cusingly, "Just whose idea was this?" and I was saying
sarcastically, "Just *whose* idea was it?" We were both
scared; and when the bus driver bellowed, "Consolidated!
Gate Two!," we had to ignore a small voice that whispered,
"Why not ride right past Gate Two?" Instead we
scrambled out into the crowd—although "crowd" doesn't
sound like as many as were in that mob. To us, it seemed
as if everybody in San Diego were headed for Gate Two,
thousands of people pushing across the over-pass which
bridged the highway, streaming out of an unending line
of buses, even leaping down the hills from parking places
half a mile away.

Quite breathless, we showed our temporary identification cards to the guard at the gate, who told us to wait
"over there." "Over there" was inside the ten foot cement
wall topped with electrically charged barbed wire which
surrounded the plant. The people who were opening their
lunch boxes for inspection as they went through the gate
looked at us curiously, probably because our uniforms were
bright and blue. We were obviously "new." (I like to
think of the way our uniforms were that first day, because
they were never that clean again all summer.)

We were joined soon by the other new employees: a

few men, one of whom was deaf, and a great many girls, both factory and office workers, distinguished only by the fact that the former were wearing slacks. As our little group grew larger, men who looked like a combination of policemen and soldiers came up to call roll and to inspect the contents of the tool boxes. They didn't bother to look at ours, which they probably thought were lunch boxes anyway. C.M. and I had just two tools apiece, battered pliers and shiny new screwdrivers which we had been instructed to bring (in a tool box) by Mrs. Hires of the Employment Office. Although the tool boxes which we had had in mind were something like sewing kits, in the end we had had to purchase two small lunch boxes, the unpleasant color of unripe green olives. C.M.'s was locked with a handsome Yale padlock, but mine was held together by a large safety pin. Thus secured within, our tools banged loudly in their loneliness.

The other girls opened huge chest-like affairs and displayed drawer after drawer of tools to the guards. We found out, by pricking our ears, that these girls were from Vocational School, where they had had a month or more of training before going on the job. They had gone to school for eight hours a day on the Swing Shift, since that was the shift they were going to work, at regular starting wages for *un*classified and *un*skilled workers — *our wages!*

The guards kept asking us our names and then checking them off the lists they carried with them. Every so often one of them would shout, "Bartholomew!" Then "C.W. Bartholomew!" And finally "Chester Winston Bartholomew?" questioningly. It was C. Winston Bartholomew we were waiting for, we decided. We had been waiting almost an hour according to the clock above the gate, and we were beginning to wonder if we would be paid for that hour. C.M. said that this Bartholomew person was probably a saboteur whose assignment from the

Gestapo was to apply for jobs in war factories and then never turn up for work. By applying for several jobs every day, he could eliminate a great many working hours. A hundred, we thought, was probably his quota for a day; and keeping C.M. and me waiting for an hour would give him two working hours to his credit. Later, when we found out how little we did that first night, we decided he should get only half credit for us.

Chester Winston Bartholomew never did turn up (naturally), and finally at 5:30 the guards took us into the Identification Bureau. There our names were checked off still another list and we were each given a large green button. C.M.'s and mine had 192 in big figures on it (that was our department number, 192, Minor Installations on the B-24, the clerk explained) and 4126 and 4042 in smaller figures (those were our clock numbers, she told us). There was one other person with 192 on her button, a pretty dark-haired girl. We introduced ourselves to her. She was Pauline Leroy, she said, and she was a school-teacher from Montana. We admitted that we were school-teachers too.

"But we won't tell on you," we offered, "if you won't tell on us."

We shook hands on it.

After we had put on our green buttons (always on the left side over the heart, the clerk instructed us; and C.M. said reminiscently, "Just like a pledge pin!"), a man wearing a bright red button led us upstairs to a small auditorium. C.M. and I grabbed seats in front (not for nothing had we taught school for four years). Then the man with the red button spun out a small speech of welcome, assuring us first that our pay had started at 4:30, so we were being paid to listen to him.

"We're *war workers*," he said, capitalizing the words with his voice, "and we're *proud* of it. No matter what

13

people on the outside say, we're on the inside and we're *proud* of it." He said several times that we were *proud* of it, aggressively, for in wartime San Diego there are only three kinds of people : the service people, the civilians, and the aircraft workers.

Hanging from the ceiling above him were models of the three Consolidated planes made at the San Diego plant. He pointed them out to us. The Coronado. The Catalina. The Liberator. C.M. and I took a good look at the Liberator so that we would recognize the next one we saw —because the next one would be the real thing. *A big bomber.*

"Now we are going to see a double feature," the man with the red button said, as if he were making a small joke.

The first picture we saw showed an airplane being built. It wasn't the least bit like those production movies we used to see during the depression to explain technological unemployment, the kind where a hundred machines, almost human, did all the work while *one* man stood by to turn them on and off. In *this* picture there were thousands of men, all doing small jobs with their hands.

"Ye Gods !" I said to C.M. "Do you think that they make airplanes by hand ?"

She whispered back that that was probably the "craft" in "aircraft."

The man with the red button apologized for the age of the picture he had shown us. It was old, three years old, and all the workers in it were men. Soon, he told us impressively, Consolidated would be hiring 80 women to every 20 men.

The second picture we saw was a jittery slide film called "The Power of a Minute," which was designed to impress upon us the fact that a war can be lost for want of a shoe. It started with the ominous ticking sound of minutes passing.

"This is Time," said a voice of doom. "Now it is, and now it is no more."

The film that followed was a nerve-racking hodge-podge of two voices interrupting each other with everything listed under "Time" in Bartlett's book of familiar quotations. When at last it ended, as we had known it would, with that creepy sundial inscription, "It is later than you think," we could feel the keen edge of Time's scythe on the back of our necks.

"What are we sitting here for?" I groaned to C.M., eager to be up and building bombers. "Why don't we *do* something?"

But instead the man with the red button introduced the Safety Director to us. The Safety Director's speech to us consisted mainly of those startling statistics issued by the National Safety Council, like the fact that the number of people killed accidentally last year was equal to the entire population of El Paso, Texas; Harrisburg, Pennsylvania, or Schenectady, New York. (I could not help thinking that Schenectady, which nobody can spell anyway, would not be much of a loss.) The Safety Director also brought to us an appropriate quotation from Lincoln, who is almost as useful as the Bible for appropriate quotations: "It is the duty of every man to protect himself and those associated with him from accidents which may result in injury or death." He climaxed this quotation by taking off the glasses which he was wearing and banging them on the table in front of him. He explained (*Bang!*) that these were safety glasses (*Bang!*), made to withstand the impact of falling objects (*Bang!*), and that the company would have a pair ground to our prescription (*Bang!*) at cost (*Bang! Bang!*).

"We must get a pair of those the first thing," said C.M. to me. "Think how impressed our kids will be when we bang our glasses on the table to call the class to order!"

After the Safety Director left, the man with the red button announced that the Women's Counselor would now say a few words — to the women only. The men filed out sheepishly, probably thinking (as we did) that we were going to hear some enlightening sidelights on the facts of life.

She impressed her gentility on our little group . . .

The Women's Counselor was an exotic creature all in black with a long bob that curled under at the ends. She tried to impress her gentility upon our little group by talking in such a low voice that nobody but C.M. and me in the front row could hear her.

She warned us not to try to do a full day's work at home before we came to work ; she told us about a special exercise devised by the company doctor to relieve cramps ; and she said that we would be allowed to work while pregnant if we had the permission of our own doctors. ("The Reproduction Line," C.M. commented to me.) She urged us to take Our Problems to Our Counselors. We would know Our Counselors, she said, because they would be the only women besides the nurses wearing skirts on the production line. C.M. and I were beginning to hate women who could wear skirts to work.

"Do you think I could insult her by asking what charm school she attended?" whispered C.M. "Or would that be too subtle?" I said I thought it would. She'd probably take it as a compliment on her charm.

A whistle blew just then, and the men, looking curious, filed back. The man with the red button, who had returned with them, explained that that was the whistle for the 6:30 rest period. Now, he said, we were to go to our own departments with the girl who had been sent for us. The girl who had been sent for us looked like a clerk, although she wore slacks. Her slacks were clean, however, and so were her hands. She was introduced to us as the secretary to Mr. Plunkett, the assistant superintendent of B-24 production.

Pauline and C.M. and I followed her across the grounds, past blackish grey-green buildings and under feathery chicken-wire camouflage nets, topped with strange little houses and dark droopy trees that cast disguising shadows over the saw-tooth roof. On our way we passed a bus stop, a tool store, a hospital, and an outside stage with "Work to Win" in red, white and blue across it. Chalked up on a big bunting-draped blackboard was a list of winners in the last company bond drawing for workers with satisfactory attendance records.

At a building with a large figure "4" on the outside, we went in, shivering expectantly.

The first thing we saw was a huge poster saying, "Leading the Invasion Are the Bombers You Build." It was a moment, really a long moment, before we realized that the dark shapes looming behind the confusion in front of us were airplanes.

"There they are!" Clara Marie and I whispered softly. "There are the *big bombers!*"

CHAPTER THREE

THERE they were — the *big bombers!* But they weren't so big as we had thought they would be. We had been told the statistics: over 320 miles an hour, 34,330 pounds when empty, 110 feet in wing span, 66 feet in length, 18 feet in height; and I had explained to C.M. that 34,330 pounds was about what 172 football players would weigh and that 66 feet was the equivalent of a whole football team laid end to end. These facts had impressed her, as things laid end to end always do; but even then she had said that they seemed a Little Small for a *big bomber.*

It wasn't that the bombers weren't big; they just weren't so big as we had expected them to be. The effect of their size was broken by the paraphernalia around them. There was a platform about six feet high under the wings and another about a foot high under the belly. In the back was a ladder leading up into an opening in the under side of the tail and in the front was one going up into the nose. People were all over the bombers, popping in and out of the nose, walking along the top of the fuselage, working on the high platforms under the wings, sticking their heads out the side windows, sliding flat under the belly, climbing up and down the ladder into the tail, ducking in and out from underneath, so that the bombers looked like sleeping Gullivers overrun by the people of Lilliput.

Mr. Plunkett's secretary led us across the tracks of the line between two bombers, which were set at an angle in something like echelon flight formation so that the tail of one almost touched the wing of the other. On the far side of the building there was another row of bombers. We followed our guide down the center aisle between the two rows. At first all of the bombers looked alike to us; then we saw that they were in different stages of completion. The ones to our left, which were coming down from the beginning of the line, were closer together than those to

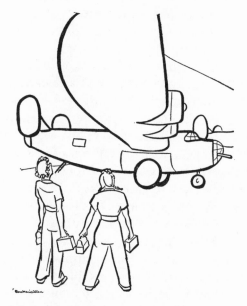

There they were — the *big bombers!*

our right, which were going up to the end, because they were still without the spreading wing-tips and tail assemblies. The bombers seemed to become more terrifying as they moved around the line, adding shiny gun turrets, huge motors, and yellow-tipped propellors; and each one looked more like an airplane than the one behind it. C.M., who dearly loves similes, said that they reminded her of giant embryos in progressive stages of pre-natal development.

"Three months," she said, pointing to the left at a sleepy-looking monster, tail-less and nose-less, with bulging eyeballs where the pilot's windows had been taped over for painting.

"Six months," I said, joining in and indicating a plane coming down the line to our right with completed tail assembly and shiny plexiglass nose and tail for the bombardier and the tail gunner.

"Nine months!" C.M. cried triumphantly, pointing to the field outside where a Liberator, four motors pounding, was being tested for delivery to the United States Army.

While C.M. and I were playing our small game, our guide passed us on to another girl, whom she introduced as Marie, the secretary to Mr. Ely, the assistant general foreman of Department 192. We wondered to ourselves who the superintendent was that Mr. Plunkett was assistant to and who the general foreman was that Mr. Ely was assistant to. We thought maybe we weren't important enough for anybody but the assistants. Later we learned that the men on the Night Shift were the "assistants" to the men in charge on the Day Shift, because if they weren't, they wouldn't work nights.

Marie was a pretty dark-haired girl with a fine posture that was displayed to advantage by her flowered long-sleeved blouse and her bright red slacks. She led us down the center aisle past time clocks, tool cribs, first aid stations, and offices; and if our eyes hadn't given us an idea of the hugeness of the B-24's, our legs certainly did, for it was a third of a mile down the line. So Marie told us.

Every so often we had to scurry to one side of the aisle to avoid a bicycle or a small truck. Once we almost walked into a large red hook just let down by the overhead crane which rolled back and forth across the ceiling. We stopped and watched with respect while the hook gently lifted a gun turret from the floor and up into the top of a plane.

As we walked down the aisle, C.M. spouted similes happily, for everything we saw looked like something else, from sleds and bells to washing machines and baby buggies. We had never seen so many things at once that we had never seen before.

At a time clock, Marie stopped and, selecting a blank card, showed us how to punch in. She pointed to the numbers on the girders above the planes and told us how to locate our position on the line by them. She explained carefully that the big number on our button was our department number and that the small one was our clock number.

"Do you have any questions?" she asked. We recognized her tone of voice, for it was the same one we use when we have just explained a difficult assignment which we know the class still doesn't understand. We didn't have any questions, probably for the same reason our class doesn't: because we didn't know which ones to ask first.

We followed Marie up a flight of stairs to an open platform office which overlooked the production line. A curly-haired man with a red button on his white shirt stood up and smiled when we came in.

"This is Mr. Ely, the assistant general foreman," Marie said. Then with a quick glance at the papers she was carrying, she added, "Miss Leroy, Mrs. Allen, Miss Bowman."

Mr. Ely smiled again (We found out later that Mr. Ely *always* smiled) and examined the papers which Marie had handed to him.

"School-teachers?" he asked, glancing up.

"School-teachers," we admitted. We hoped that he

hadn't *guessed* by the way we looked, but we thought keeping our profession a secret was going to be a little difficult if it were written all over our records.

C.M. and I told him we would work until September, and Pauline said that she would stay on if she liked the job. School teaching must be pretty bad in Montana.

Mr. Ely, scrutinizing our records carefully, next discovered the states in which we were born.

"Missouri," he said to me approvingly. "I know some fine people in Missouri."

For the rest of the summer I was "the girl from Missouri," although I had not even been in Missouri since I was five years old ; but "where you are from" is your first identification on the production line. Pauline was "the girl from Montana" and C.M. was "the native daughter." She was quite a curiosity.

Having now disposed of the social amenities, Mr. Ely asked if we had any tools. Pauline said no, but C.M. and I timidly brought forth our lunch boxes, which looked even more collapsible in the harsh practicality of the factory than they had in the basement of Sears-Roebuck. We each took out our battered pair of pliers and our bright new screwdriver. Mr. Ely smiled, a sad smile this time, and said encouragingly that that was very good but he thought we would need more tools.

"And you'll *want* to buy a tool box," he smiled.

"But these are tool boxes !" we wailed.

Mr. Ely smiled.

He too explained to us that the big number on our button was our department number and the small one was our clock number. He told us how to punch the time clock, and he showed us how to locate ourselves by the numbers above the planes. ("Ships," Mr. Ely called them.) That we would lose ourselves in the wilds of the production line seemed to be Mr. Ely's greatest fear. He warned us that

23

one new employee had lost himself for two hours when he forgot the number of the "ship" he was working in.

"Now do you have any questions?" Mr. Ely smiled. We didn't ask any this time, for none of our questions seemed important enough to ask the assistant general foreman.

Pleased that we had no questions, Mr. Ely introduced us formally to Mr. Billings, the foreman, as "Miss Leroy, Mrs. Allen, and Miss Bowman." Mr. Billings took us down the stairs again, explaining carefully as he did so that the big number on our button was our department number (We were beginning to realize that it was!) and the small one was our clock number. He showed us how to punch the time clock at the bottom of the stairs, and he pointed out the numbers above the planes. (Mr. Billings also called them "ships.")

Mr. Billings looked like a little boy, mainly because the sleeves of his blue shirt were cut off above the elbow; but he talked slowly and pompously. For an ex-school teacher, which we found out later he was, Mr. Billings' psychology was bad. We had come to build bombers, but he acted as if we had come to make men.

"I do not allow any dating whatsoever on company time," he said sternly. "A man and a woman cannot work together and date at the same time," he added wisely. We smiled sweetly and obediently, although the girl from Montana whispered to me that there wasn't a man on the line she'd be seen dead with, including Mr. B. himself. (Later in the summer, however, we saw her out on dates with men from the plant, and she didn't look dead to us.)

Mr. Billings looked critically at our hair, mine fluffy in a victory bob, C.M.'s in pig-tails, and Pauline's in a mane at her neck.

"I do not allow girls to work without hair coverings," Mr. Billings stated emphatically. We mentally counted

24

the girls we could see who were working *without* hair coverings : nine out of fourteen ; and we decided that Mr. B's. bark had no bite.

"Do you have any tools ?" Mr. Billings wanted to know.

We admitted that we had, and we shamefacedly opened our tool boxes to show him the pliers and the screwdrivers. He looked disapprovingly at them and said that we would need *many* more tools.

"And you'll *want* to buy a tool box," he said, holding our little boxes so disdainfully that they seemed to cringe in his grasp.

"We're going to work *only* two months," C.M. objected, but Mr. Billings ignored her objection.

"This is a real job," he said, looking up at the B-24's and talking in the embarrassed gruff manner of a football coach before the big game. "It's the way I earn my living —although that isn't important because I could earn my living some other way. The important thing is that I have two brothers out there, flying these ships. And I'm here to see that they get the ships to fly." He paused.

"Do you have any questions ?" he asked abruptly. We said no, we didn't, for our questions seemed unimportant after Mr. Billings' speech.

He turned then and introduced us to two young men who had come up while he was talking.

"Mrs. Allen, Mr. Tompkinson," he said. "Mr. Tompkinson will be your leadman, Mrs. Allen. And Miss Bowman and Miss Leroy, Mr. MacGregor."

After he had introduced us, Mr. Billings left.

Mr. MacGregor was a lean lad in a khaki shirt with a low slung belt that made me wonder how he kept his trousers up. (I finally decided that the trousers must keep the belt up.) He had "Leadman" printed down the side of his button, but it was green like ours, not red like Mr. Billings' and Mr. Ely's. While he was talking to Pauline and me, he absent-mindedly dusted his work bench and arranged the things on it in neat rows. He too explained that the big number on our button was our department number and the small one was our clock number. He told us how to punch the time clock, and he showed us how to locate ourselves by the numbers above the planes. ("Ships," said Mr. MacGregor.) I could hear Mr. Tompkinson, who was also a lean lad with a low slung belt (*all* leadmen were!), explaining to C.M. about the button and the time clock and the numbers above the "ships."

"Do you have any questions?" asked Mr. MacGregor, and I heard an echo from Mr. Tompkinson.

"Yes!" Pauline and I said together, and I saw C.M.'s mouth opening too. "What——"

The rest of the question we didn't hear ourselves because the lunch whistle blew at the same time that we asked it. Mr. MacGregor and Mr. Tompkinson didn't hear the rest of the question either. By the time the whistle stopped blowing, they were half way down the production line with their lunch boxes under their arms.

I turned to C.M.

"Do you have any questions?" I asked, with an expression of expectant interest.

"Yes!" she said. "I know that the big number on my button is my department number and the small one is my clock number. I know how to punch the time clock, and I understand about the numbers above the planes." She stopped for breath. "What I want to know is," she said plaintively, *"what are we going to do?"*

CHAPTER FOUR

AFTER lunch C.M. disappeared down the line with Mr. Tompkinson and Pauline and I climbed up into the ship in front of Station 20 with Mr. MacGregor. (I was making a point of noting the station numbers, as instructed by Mr. Ely, Mr. Billings, and Mr. MacGregor.) I thought that I had not seen so much shiny new metal since Pearl Harbor. The inside of the tail section where we were looked like a covered wagon made out of my mother's best cookie tin. (There was one small door made of wood, "to save metal," Mr. MacGregor explained, which just goes to show with what careful attention the aircraft industry watches the smallest details.)

Mr. MacGregor stepped over and around the people who were working in the tail section, and Pauline and I followed him, saying "Pardon me" politely to everyone. Mr. MacGregor waved his hand carelessly at this and that, and said that this was a such-and-such and that did so-and-so. Pauline and I looked earnestly at everything he indicated.

He took a great deal of time to explain to us that the large and small ribs which spanned the ship were called bulkheads and beltframes. The large ones were the bulkheads, he told us, and they divided the ship into its main sections. Then locations of installations could be stated by the number of the bulkhead and the beltframe. For instance, 7.4-7.5 (which was printed on the cover of a tiny window near the floor of the ship) was between the fourth and fifth beltframes after the seventh bulkhead. This bit of information seemed very useful to Pauline and me; and we made a great point of remembering it, but never once this summer did Mr. MacGregor dispatch us to make a certain installation at a certain beltframe.

Most of Mr. MacGregor's explanations we lost in the screaming, pounding rattle of a rivet gun at the very end of the tail. The girl who was using it seemed to be working very industriously, as did everybody else in the ship. A round-faced man, who looked like Peter Lorre and sounded like Bing Crosby, was doing something with some small pipes over our heads while he hummed "Home on the Range." A girl, wearing the sort of a sweater which makes some factories prohibit the wearing of sweaters, was poking a bundle of thin wires through a hole in the beltframe above the window. A blond boy who said "Excuse me" without looking up was stringing a cable along the floor. Their industry impressed me, but we found out later that it was mainly to impress Mr. MacGregor, for he was also their leadman.

I got a little dizzy when I looked out of the window of the plane, because inside we were square with everything and outside everything was at an angle to us. Once I even let out a small yelp when I looked down and thought I saw the floor moving away. I had a horrible feeling that somebody had made a mistake and our plane was actually flying off the production line, unfinished as it was. Then I looked again and saw that a big platform had just been rolled past below us. I subsided into an embarrassed silence.

Mr. MacGregor, pointing out the sights as he went, led us up toward the front of the ship. This was where the belly turret went. That was where the life raft was stored. That was the command deck. He ducked down through a tiny door and onto a narrow cat-walk, and we squeezed through after him. This was the bomb bay, where the bombs were stored, he explained, turning sidewise to go between the two racks on either side and lifting his feet gingerly over the boxes and cans and motors that were set along the cat-walk. He pointed toward the front of the bomb bay. That was the under-flight deck. That was the flight deck. That was where the pilot sat. That was where the radio man sat. Pauline asked him where the navigator sat.

"A boy friend?" inquired Mr. MacGregor, and she said shyly yes.

I dutifully tried to remember where Mr. MacGregor had said that the pilot sat and the co-pilot and the radio man and the navigator, but I couldn't. I couldn't even remember which was the flight deck and which was the command deck. I was sure I could never find my way back into the bomb bay again. It was much later that I finally figured it all out with the aid of a diagram which C.M. made for me. C.M. has the visual mind. She is the kind of person who studies the maps in detective stories, which I always ignore. But here is the diagram, since a diagram is better than description to show you the location of all the places where we later worked in the *big bombers*.

After Mr. MacGregor had shown us through the ship, he took us back to Station 20. That was his station, he told us, and we would "work out" of it. He pointed out on the chart above the bench, which wasn't a bench at all but a table, the list of installations made by his station. The ships were listed across the top of the chart and divided into alternate groups between the Night Shift and the Day Shift so that a quick glance at the chart told everybody in Station 20 on which ship he was to start work each night.

"Now *this* will be your installation," Mr. MacGregor said to me, "and *this* will be yours," to Pauline; and he pointed to the two installations listed at the bottom of the chart.

After he had placed Pauline under the care of a quiet, pale girl who was to show her how to put in something referred to by Mr. MacGregor as "the black stuff," he turned his full attention to me.   First he asked me if I had any tools.   He looked disgusted when I showed the two of them to him.

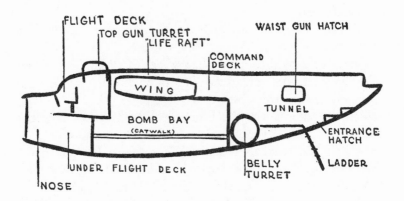

"You'll need more tools," he said, fingering my pliers and screwdriver disdainfully.   "And you'll *want* to buy a tool box."

I knew that I wouldn't *want* to buy a tool box; but cowed by his scowl, I said yes, I would.   He said he would lend me the tools I needed for that night, but I would have to have my own the next night.   He thoughtfully dictated a little list of nine to me.

"Now come with me," he said.

I trailed him across the line of ships to a row of shelves where small parts were kept in what looked like deep cake pans.   From these, Mr. MacGregor selected several bright green rollers and an equal number of triangular metal pieces.   He deposited them in a large paper bag which he gave to me to carry while he led the way to the "crib," a little caged storeroom.

"A and N 4 dash 5 bolts and low castellated nuts," ordered Mr. MacGregor, "and cotter keys, 2 dash 2."

"With or without ?" asked the clerk.

"With," said Mr. MacGregor. (I found out later that he meant *with* holes.) "Now remember those," he told me, "so that you can get your own tomorrow."

I dutifully recited to myself, "An A and N bolt, 4 dash 5, and an A and N nut, low castellated." I wondered what a castellated nut was ; it turned out to be one with a back like the top of a castle battlement. At the end of the evening I could still remember the numbers (in fact, I have never forgotten them,) but I soon found out that I was the only person who ever asked for bolts and nuts by name and number at the crib. Everybody else brought a sample of what he wanted.

Back at the bench, Mr. MacGregor put me to work with the materials he had gathered. Assembling and installing safety belt holders was to be my own private job, he explained ; and if I were absent, he told me impressively, the safety belt holders would not go into the ships. I wondered how long the B-24's would be allowed to go off the line without them, but I discovered later that somebody else would take over the job if I missed more than a day. Mr. MacGregor asked me how I thought I would like my job and I said fine, not having the faintest idea.

Assembling the safety belt holders turned out to be a complex job — for me, since it involved the use of five different tools and my previous experience with tools had been limited to a hammer and a thumb tack remover. First Mr. MacGregor handed me an unfamiliar little instrument, the handle of which he flipped with a clicking noise.

"Here," he said, "untighten this bolt."

The English teacher in me shuddered at the use of "untighten" (I did not know that I would be using the word myself in a few weeks!), and I shuddered at the thought of using this strange instrument, especially since I was not quite sure which was the bolt and which was the nut. I looked at it vaguely and said meekly to Mr. MacGregor, "Please, will you show me how to use it?" I could hear something inside him saying "Women!" disgustedly as he expertly manipulated what I later learned was a ratchet. Next he handed me a fiendish looking weapon that trailed a length of electric cord and resembled a pregnant pistol.

"Here," he ordered, setting six metal triangles in the vise, "drill a hole through these pieces." I bravely stuck the point against the first triangle, although I could practically see the thing, whatever it was, flying to pieces in my hand. I clutched it as hard as I could, squeezed the trigger, and *prayed*. The point whirled around faster and faster, vibrating so hard that I began to wonder if I were being electrocuted. Just as I decided that I was, it snapped through the final piece with a suddenness that shook me. Mr. MacGregor looked at the holes, which had a strange oblong shape, and said begrudgingly that he guessed they would do.

He next showed me how to un-screw and re-screw half of the little rollers so that they could go on the left-hand side of the ship. They were all made for the right-hand side, he explained, because the Parts Plant didn't know which side they were to go on. This seemed like a waste of time to me, as I told Mr. MacGregor politely, because why couldn't half of the holders be made for the right side of the ship and half for the left. They were always installed in pairs anyway. Mr. MacGregor said that he for one didn't know, but that was the Parts Plant for you! I did not know then that all of the trouble on the Night Shift which wasn't caused by the bungling inefficiency of the Day Shift was brought about by the utter stupidity of the Parts Plant.

Mr. MacGregor left me at last with my tools and my motor and a dozen safety belt holders to assemble. As I tentatively poised my screwdriver, Mr. Ely came by.

"How do you like it?" smiled Mr. Ely.

I said fine, although I did think I would know better after I had tightened my first bolt. After Mr. Ely left, I tightened my first bolt quite nicely except for the fact that I put it in backwards. While I was taking it out, Mr. Billings came up.

"How do you like it now?" asked Mr. Billings.

I said fine and tried to look as if I were taking out a bolt that somebody else had put in backwards.

Mr. MacGregor's plan had been that after I had assembled a half dozen pairs of safety belt holders, he would take me up into a ship and show me how to install them. The only trouble with this plan was that some new and difficult installation was being made by Station 20 that night and every few minutes Mr. MacGregor would come wearily and worriedly back to the bench and tell me to assemble a few more holders.

"How do you like it?" he would ask each time and then hurry off to a conference with Mr. Ely and Mr. Billings as I said fine.

The result was that by the time the quitting whistle blew at one o'clock, I was practically hidden behind *dozens* and *dozens* of safety belt holders. That was all right though, Mr. MacGregor told me when he came back, because then I wouldn't have to assemble any more for a few days. He gave me strict orders to *hide* all of them I had done under the bench. I did not quite understand why it was necessary to hide them. The next night when I discovered that all my painstakingly assembled holders were gone, I understood. The Day Shift had found my secret hiding place under the bench and had taken my completed holders for their own ships. *That* was the Day Shift for you.

A few minutes after the whistle blew, C.M. turned up, searching forlornly for her tool box, which she was afraid somebody had put in with the lunch boxes by mistake. She looked so worried that several people asked her if she were lost. Whenever we looked bewildered (which was quite often, because everything was bewildering), somebody always came up and inquired sympathetically, "Are

He told me to assemble a few more . . .

you lost?" When we finally found C.M.'s tool box, which was among the lunch boxes as we had suspected it would be, we gathered up our possessions and marched bravely off to the time clock — bravely because we had never punched a time clock before.

C.M. told me that she had been working in the bomb bay, actually in a *big bomber*. She was very superior about having been allowed to work in a ship while I had been kept at the bench. When I *finally* pinned her down though, she admitted that she had just been tying strings around the wires and the only difficult thing about the job was a knot known as "the electrician's hitch" which she had not yet mastered. (She reminded me before I could say anything that *she* had not had any difficulty at all with the square knot in First Aid, the intricacies of which had completely baffled me.) I put C.M. in her place by pointing out that I had a job all to myself, a *responsibility*, and she was merely a helper to someone else.

"If I don't put the safety belt holders in, they won't go in," I said proudly.

"Then they probably won't go in," said C.M. nastily as we arrived at the time clock.

Just as if she punched a time clock every night, she speedily glanced over the "Out" cards for hers. Then she started over, slowly, scrutinizing each one carefully.

"That's the 'Out' side," said the timekeeper with a pleasant smile. "Your card will be on the 'In' side."

"But we're going *out,*" objected C.M.

"But you're *in* now," pointed out the timekeeper.

We shifted our search embarrassedly to the "In" side, where we quickly found our cards because they were the only ones left in the rack. We slipped them into the slot at the top of the time clock and there was a gentle bong as we pulled the lever down. On the back of each card was stamped the time: 1:10. The timekeeper watched us carefully to see that we put our cards in the "Out" rack.

"How do you like it?" she asked us.

We said fine.

Everybody asked us how we liked it as we went out. Their pleasant friendliness was disarming.

"How's everything?" said the man who looked like Peter Lorre.

"How do you like it now?" smiled Mr. Ely.

"How are you doing?" asked the girl in The Sweater.

"How do you like it now?" said Mr. Billings.

"How do you like it?" asked the guard at the gate.

We said we liked it fine—and come to think about it, we did.

CHAPTER FIVE

IF there was one night this summer that C.M. and I were ready to quit, it was our second night on the job. The second night was like the second day with a new class when they try you out, or the second day with a new teacher when she gets down to work.

The first night Mr. MacGregor had explained things slowly and twice as if I were a not-too-bright child. He had offered to lend me his own tools, and he had been pleasantly encouraging when I accomplished some small task satisfactorily. But the second night! The second night he expected me to remember *everything* he had told me the night before, and he was positively disgusted that I had not been able to purchase my tools, although as I pointed out to him it was as difficult to buy tools in San Diego as to buy nylon stockings or whitewall tires. At least, when I asked the clerk at the hardware store for a midget ratchet set, she looked at me curiously and said didn't I know there was a war on.

Mr. MacGregor grumbled, but he lent his tools to me and put me to work assembling more safety belt holders to replace those that the Day Shift had stolen. When I had completed a small pile, he showed me how to install them actually in the ships, two holders to each ship, five holes drilled in each holder, and a bolt and a nut for each hole. Mr. MacGregor intimated that the job was simplicity itself, and he put up a pair of holders himself to show me how. It took him practically no time at all.

37

"Do these ships tonight," he said, scratching down a list of numbers and carelessly dumping assorted bolts and nuts into the thermos compartment of my little tool box. "And if you make a mistake, *tell* me about it."

That was his parting instruction. It seemed it was the policy of the company, as announced on signs all over the plant, to forgive a worker his sins if he confessed them. The one unforgivable sin was "covering up" a mistake.

After Mr. MacGregor left me, I squatted on the floor of the ship and carefully measured and marked little crosses where the five holes were to be drilled on each side. I measured twice *to be sure*. Then I got down on my knees, gritted my teeth, clutched the electric motor, and pressed its point to the center of the first cross. Zip! It sassily slid off the mark, leaving a tiny chewed up trail behind it. The second time it slid off in the same direction. The third time it slid off in a new direction. The fourth time it made a spiral. The fifth time I put all my strength behind it and *pushed*. It went through suddenly, and I banged my head soundly on the metal sill above me. The second hole was easier, although it ended up more like an oval than a circle. The third hole was lonesomely out of line with the other two, and the fourth was too close to the third. The last hole was an achievement, to my mind at least, although I took so long to drill it that someone asked kindly, "Is your drill dull?"

I stood up, my knees cracking embarrassingly as I did so, and bent over to put in the bolts and nuts. Then I sat down on the floor to tighten them. I hoped the exercise would be good for my figure. I had read an article once about how your job can be a setting-up exercise for beauty.

I surveyed my five bolts, which were in a rather informal line like soldiers at ease, and turned to the other side of the ship. I squatted, I kneeled, I bent straight from the hips,

I sat on the floor. Mr. MacGregor looked up into the ship and said that my bolts were *not* in a straight line, which observation I thought was a masterpiece of understatement.

While I was going through my own inexpert version of "The Turn of the Screwdriver" in the next ship, Mr. Billings stuck his head up through the hatch. I was taking such a painfully long time that he climbed in and tightened the rest of the bolts for me. He also pulled my now dented tool box out of the corner where somebody had kicked it and looked sadly at my collection of bolts and nuts in the thermos compartment.

"You'll *want* to buy a tool box," Mr. Billings said again.

He seemed to be under the impression that I would be investing much money in tools (That was what *he* thought!) and that the tool box would pay for itself because otherwise, he told me confidently, all my tools would be lost or stolen. I thought obstinately that I didn't intend to invest enough money in tools to make them worth stealing, but I didn't tell Mr. Billings so. He also seemed to be of the opinion that my own box would collapse at the slightest pressure, thus dumping my bolts and nuts all over the floor. In this opinion he was quite right; in the next ship when Mr. Ely looked up and smiled sympathetically, I was on my hands and knees gathering up my bolts and nuts.

While I had been squatting, kneeling, bending, and sitting on the floor in the tail section of the ship, C.M. had been stretching in the bomb bay, boggling and clipping the electric wires which would later release the bombs.

"Boggle-boggle, clip-clip!" she kept repeating at intervals during lunch, giving the phrase a hot jive inflection. A boggle, I finally got out of her, was a piece of vitylite which protected the wires where they came in contact with sharp edges, and a clip was a small metal band with which the wires were attached to the side of the ship.

C.M.'s "routine" in her corner of the bomb bay was two boggles and then two clips. "Boggle-boggle, clip-clip."

I told her about making her job a setting-up exercise for beauty because I thought that stretching would be fine for the bust and for the chin. C.M. agreed enthusiastically and said that she could do her exercises for strengthening her eyes, building up her arches, and making her features more expressive as well.

At lunch-time we also compared notes on our tools and our tool boxes. C.M., it seemed, had been marched off by Mr. Tompkinson, her leadman, to the company tool store to purchase the tools she needed. That was the trouble with "wimen workers," according to Mr. T.——they never wanted to buy tools. His original list for C.M. had included eight tools, but in a bitter struggle she had cut it down to two by insisting that she was sure she could dig the others up at home. (And dig them up she did—or at least they looked as if they had been dug up, for they bore the patina of archeological remains.) She told me proudly that she had put her foot down on the tool box, and I said that that was just the trouble with mine : somebody had put his foot down on it. We both said that by golly, we were not going to buy another tool box (Mr. Billings to the contrary notwithstanding), that one dollar and one cent with the tax was enough for any tool box for only two months' work, and that we privately thought Mr. B. collected a commission on every one he sold anyway.

After lunch, however, Mr. MacGregor, who hadn't forgotten about my tools either, dispatched me with a list of six to find Mr. Billings and get an O.K. on the purchase. Mr. Billings looked the list over approvingly and added *TOOL BOX* in capital letters. He then gave me a glass slab with "Tool Purchase Permit" printed on it in large letters. I held this helplessly at first, not quite sure what I was supposed to do with it ; then I decided to display it like a banner as I marched down to the tool store so that no one would think I was going to get a drink, or wash my hands, or visit a friend in another department.

At the tool store there was a large sign that said, "Tools are the weapons at home. Do you know that tools are *scarce ?*" I hoped that the tools I was supposed to buy were so scarce that they would not be available ; but they weren't, except the midget ratchet set. "Midget ratchet set" is a fine phrase to roll on the tongue, but one of them costs so much money that their scarcity was a pleasant surprise to me.

The clerk asked me if I wanted my bill taken out of my pay, and if so, out of how many checks. I said gloomily that he could take it all out of the first one, if he could get that much out of it. Then I marched back to Station 20 with my new tool box and my new tools. I saw Mr. Ely on the way and he smiled. I saw Mr. Billings too and he looked very pleased. At Station 20, Mr. MacGregor inspected my purchases and said that I had made a *good start.*

After I got my tool box, I felt much more professional because people stopped looking at me curiously as if I were carrying my lunch box from ship to ship. When I found out that the box was useful to sit on, I felt more kindly toward Mr. Billings. But I did have much difficulty climbing up the ladder into the tail with my motor in one hand and my tool box in the other. This, if I had realized it, was not a difficult feat at all because a few days later I was climbing the same ladder with not only the motor and the tool box but also a small stool, an electric light enclosed in a little wire cage, and assorted parts of the most awkward shapes the engineering department was able to design.

Sometimes now I wonder that in my ignorance and awkwardness that second night I didn't kill someone. Once I did ingratiate myself with the administration and endear myself to my fellow workers when I dropped my drill motor down the hatch and narrowly missed the assistant foreman's head. Slightly shaken, the assistant foreman picked it up and handed it back to me. I said that I was sorry while I wondered what I would have said if it had actually landed on his head. The other people working in the ship were mightily pleased. They said that the assistant foreman was a *slave driver,* and it was a pity I had missed him. That was before I had learned that "slave driver" was practically a synonym for "foreman" in the vocabulary of the workers on the production line.

By the time that the quitting whistle blew at one o'clock, I had installed safety belt holders in all the ships on Mr. MacGregor's list. (If you're flying a B-24, you'll recognize mine because they are the crooked ones.) For every holder I had installed, I had squatted, kneeled, bent, and sat on the floor. I had gritted my teeth, clutched my motor, and pushed as hard as I could push. I had stubbed my toes, cracked my shins, and knocked my head three times on the metal sill above the safety belt holders. I had broken my fingernails, I had cut my fingers, and once I had almost bitten through my tongue, which in moments of stress I stick out and curl around my right check.

At one o'clock, I was tireder than I have ever been in my life — and also dirtier. My hair was tinseled with tiny shavings of metal, my hands were grimy, and my fingernails were bordered in black. My face was shiny through the smudges, my hair was tousled, and my lipstick was gone. My uniform, my bright blue uniform of yesterday afternoon, had a tear in the knee, a streak of grease across the blouse, and a large dusty circle on the seat of the pants where I had sat on the floor.

C.M., I was pleased to see, looked every bit as tired and dirty as I did. Together we hobbled down to the time clock while spry grey-haired women twice our age briskly passed us. Buck, the girl who delivered the electrical materials to the bomb bay where C. M. worked, stopped to tell us that one night she had clocked herself on a pedometer strapped to her ankle, and she'd found out that she had walked twelve miles during her eight hours at work that night.

"Do your feet hurt?" she asked sympathetically.

C.M. said she didn't know; she hadn't looked lately to see whether they were her feet or just the bloody ends.

On our way out to the gate (It was only a mere quarter of a mile!) we passed the pavilion where the Work-to-Win bond drawings were held each month.

"By golly," said C.M., "if I ever win the $1000 bond, I'm going to take it and say, 'Thank you, I'm terminating!'"

We agreed that if either of us won it, or even one of the $500 bonds, we'd split it between us and both terminate. ("Terminate" in aircraft language means to quit, resign, or otherwise end employment.) At that particular moment, I am ashamed to say, we had completely lost our enthusiasm for building bombers and winning the war. We found out later that all women workers felt the same way on their second aching night of work — and many of them did terminate. One girl who had come in with our own group quit after an hour and twenty minutes on the job.

"She thought it was too hard after Vacational School," drawled Emeline, C.M.'s partner in the bomb bay.

At first, we thought that Vacational School was a pun for Vocational School, where women workers got prefactory training which they scorned as "a waste of time." Later we realized that it was merely an oddly appropriate mispronunciation. It was not surprising that, for some women, the contrast between learning and working (at the same rate of pay) seemed too great.

C.M. and I, still dreaming of winning the $1000 bond, showed our lunch boxes to the guard at the gate and wearily dragged ourselves up the steps of the over-pass which led to the bus stop on the other side. These steps had been engineered for the maximum discomfort to tired aircraft workers like us. As C.M. said, most steps are either too short or too high—but these were both. They were built high so that signs like "Positively No Sitting on Steps" could be painted on them. As if anybody could sit on those steps!

It felt as good as an overstuffed lounge.

At the bus stop we stood while the other women sat comfortably on the curbstone, their lunch boxes between their knees. I looked longingly at them and tentatively at C.M., but she was standing straight and composed, like a lady with standards who would never sit on the curb to wait for a bus — no matter how much her neck and arms and back and legs and knees and feet did ache. So I didn't say anything.

Finally she turned to me.

"Do you think — ?" she began, looking at the women on the curb. "Do you think that maybe —— ?"

"Yes !" I said.

And we sat down on the curb, which felt as good as an overstuffed lounge to us at that moment.

It was two o'clock when at last we reached C.M.'s. We threw ourselves limply on the couch, C.M. with a letter from Fred, her husband.

I didn't think I was ever going to be able to get up again. I had a lumpy feeling of bruises and knotted muscles. My right hand wouldn't quite close, and the little finger was perfectly numb. The tips of all my fingers felt smooth. I asked C.M. if she thought I still had fingerprints. She looked up from her letter and said that probably I didn't so why didn't I try to crack a safe the way Jimmy Valentine used to.

"Remember how we used to shiver when he sandpapered the ends of his fingers to make them sensitive ?" she asked.

"Sandpapering isn't necessary !" I groaned as C.M. returned to her letter from Fred.

"Fred says he's glad to hear we're not going to eat after work," she told me. "He says we ought to lose ten pounds apiece this summer. He says — *oooooh !*" she shrieked, sitting up so suddenly that my own bones creaked in sympathy. "He says *why don't we take setting-up exercises this summer ?*"

CHAPTER SIX

C.M. said positively that no night, absolutely no night, could ever be as bad as the second night on the job had been. But the third night was. So was the fourth night. And the fifth night.

When we took our aches and pains to the nurse in First Aid, she asked us if our jobs involved the use of unfamiliar tools or unused muscles. We had to admit that to us all tools were unfamiliar and all muscles unused.

"Oh, well, then," she said confidently, "you'll get used to it."

Everybody on the line said we'd get used to it, but we said there were some things we'd never get used to — creaking like a rusty hinge, for instance, and feeling like the walking dead.

"You'll get used to it," everybody said. "I did."

But on the last day of our first week, we were still not used to it. We started out for work unwillingly because it was hot, it was the middle of the afternoon, and it was a hell of a time to be going to work. We approached Gate Two as if it had "Abandon Hope, All Ye Who Enter Here" blazoned in blood above it. We looked at our fellow workers as if they were wax dummies in a show window. Since we felt, at this particular time of the afternoon, that they did not exist at all and we ourselves were invisible, we were amazed when they recognized us and said hello. With the eyes of strangers, we observed them, our fellow workers, squinting into the sun, looking tired already, eating the unattractive foods which they had purchased at the little mobile commissaries inside the gates.

It was a hell of a time to be going to work.

They were a depressed looking lot, and they had the worst posture in the world. "The Aircraft Worker's Slouch," C.M. and I had christened it, guiltily pulling our own tummies in. We considered it the greatest occupational hazard on the production line. Every job was either so low that we had to slump into a reverse "S" with concave chest and convex abdomen to reach it, or so high that we had to climb on a stool and then bend down to reach it. Every "short" job was delegated to a tall person, and vice versa, so that regular giants were squeezed into the life raft compartment, folded up in the under flight deck, or wedged between the oxygen bottles on the command deck ;

and virtual midgets were straddling the hatch entrance to the tail section, one foot on top of the door and the other on the hand railing that ran along the other side. Every platform was carefully adjusted so that no human being of normal size could pass under it standing straight, but instead had to walk like a gorilla, feet flat, arms dangling, and neck sunk into his shoulders. It was already our opinion (and experience) that slipping into the Aircraft Worker's Slouch was unavoidable on the production line ; besides it was the only way we could keep our stretching, bagging, drooping slacks from falling off.

This particular afternoon we entered Building Four which was relatively quiet and empty between shifts, as if it were a mausoleum. We looked haughtily at a Red Button who was conferring with a small group of men. (It was amazing how soon, as Labor, we had developed a slight antagonism toward Management.) We looked curiously at a member of the Day Shift who was putting in over-time until 5 :0. He looked like a swing shifter, but that just shows you never can tell.

At the time clock rack, we reached for our cards as if we were doing something against our better judgment. The Day Shift timekeeper, who was putting his cards back into the "Out" rack, looked apprehensively at me because one afternoon I had punched a Day Shift card by mistake. C.M. picked her card out of the rack with the airy nonchalance of a magician selecting the ace of spades from a deck of cards. Then she patronizingly reached for mine as she had reached for hers — and drew out the wrong card. Hers was always easy to find because it was off by itself while mine was right in the middle of the largest group of cards. Quietly enraged by her unasked-for assistance, I painstakingly checked back through the numbers on the cards until I came to 4042. Then I made sure that it belonged to C.H. Bowman before I punched it. The Day Shift timekeeper, who had stopped putting in his cards for a moment, looked relieved.

The gentle bong of the time clock had a strange effect on C.M. and me, for the moment we heard it we unaccountably lost that strange visitor-from-Mars feeling. Things were to be done, and we had to do them. We both had to equip ourselves with motors, lights, and stools for our night's work in the ships. Quickly we grabbed our lunch boxes and marched back down the line to Station 20, which was placed tantalizingly opposite the spot where we had entered the building on our way to the time clock. (Sometimes it didn't seem quite fair that our building should be the one farthest from the gate and our time clock should be the one farthest from the entrance to the building.)

As soon as we started down the line, C.M. began to dart nervous glances at the platform under the bomb bay of every ship we passed ; and whenever we passed one with a particularly generous collection of motors, lights, and stools left on it by the Day Shift, she insisted that we had better get our things right there instead of waiting until we got down to Station 20 where there might not be any. I *knew* that everything we needed would be in the bomb bay of the ship in front of Station 20 ; it had been every night that we had carted motors, lights, and stools all the way from Station 27 to 20—and I told C.M. so.

"We-e-ell," C.M. said unwillingly, casting an envious glance back at the crowded bomb bay of the ship at 27 as she followed me down the line.

Unfortunately, this particular night, the only night this summer that I bullied C.M. into waiting until we got to Station 20, the bomb bay in the ship there was completely deserted. Not a motor. Not a light. Not a stool. C.M. didn't say *anything*. She just folded her arms and stood, tapping her foot ominously. I sheepishly inspected the bomb bay opposite Station 21 — deserted. Station 22 — deserted. I walked back to Station 23. Station 24. Station 25. 26. 27. I selected the sturdiest stool available, disregarding those cushioned with an intricate arrangement of adhesive tape which C.M. and I used to pick out at first for their comfortable over-stuffed look until we discovered that the tape was put on primarily to keep them from disintegrating into a million toothpicks. I also selected a light, untangling the cord and following it through to its plug, passing it up and over and around and under all the others. Then I lifted up a floorboard to see if the Day Shift had hidden a motor there. They had. And since any motor that was considered worth hiding was bound to be good, I took it.

Selecting a motor was usually a problem, for we often discovered that the motor we had picked out and carried back to Station 20 wobbled madly when we started to use it, didn't work at all, or gave us a mild, and sometimes not so mild, electric shock. The other woman who was gathering her equipment at 27 told me she had received a shock from each of the two motors she had tested that afternoon. One more and she was going to terminate right then and there, she told me emphatically.

"I'm allergic to electricity," she explained. "It runs in my family. My uncle was electrocuted."

"That must have been quite a shock," I murmured sympathetically.

I gathered up my equipment and returned to Station 20. C.M. still looked displeased. (I mention this rather painful matter only because it explains why we always carried our equipment from Station 27 to Station 20 for the rest of the summer.)

There was a girl I had not seen before sitting on the bench at Station 20 with her legs folded up under her. C.M. and I said hello and she said hello, forlornly.

50

"How long have you been here?" I asked. I had learned that that was the accepted opening for a conversation on the production line, even before "Where are you from?"

"Four days today," she said unhappily. "How long have you been here?"

"A *week* today," I said proudly. I felt very experienced.

"You'll get used to it," C.M. assured the girl from the wealth of *her* experience.

I looked at C.M. in amazement. Just then the warning whistle blew. Hundreds of people appeared carrying tool boxes, stools, lights, and motors; I don't know where they all came from. Everybody scanned the chart above the bench and counted off the ships to find out which were the Night Shift's. Somebody let down the ladders leading into the tail, which had been hooked up a few inches above the floor for moving of the ships between shifts. Mr. Ely and Mr. Billings walked past Station 20. The lights went on in the ships. Another whistle blew. There was a sound of riveting, drilling, and hammering.

"What did you say to that girl?" I demanded of C.M. as we started down the line to the ships we had finished in the night before.

"I said she'd get used to it," she answered defensively. "And she will!"

C.M. was right. The girl would get used to it — for suddenly, we had.

CHAPTER SEVEN

On the Wednesday that marked the end of our first week on the production line C.M. said that we should write a chapter about what an ordinary night at work was like. I objected that we had worked only six nights and five of those hadn't been ordinary at all. That was all right, C.M. insisted stubbornly; one ordinary night was *enough* because all the other ordinary nights would be just like it. Beaten down by this irrefutable logic, I agreed to write the seventh chapter about an *ordinary* night on the production line.

Such an ordinary night began when the whistle blew at 4:30 with somebody saying as he slid unwillingly off the bench, "Only eight and a half more hours until one o'clock." The men and women on the line were as conscious of time as a child in the classroom. They knew exactly to the week how long they had worked at Consolidated. At first this amazed C.M. and me, for when someone asked us suddenly how long we had taught school the answer always involved some complex subtraction of September, 1939, or was it 1940?, from the present date. But even after only a week at Consolidated, we knew that Wednesday night would always be an anniversary. Three weeks tonight, we would say, or four, or five.

"It's like a jail sentence," the fat boy who tested the radio equipment on the command deck explained to me, "and after the war, we'll be out."

"No lie," agreed the girl who was stringing a cable behind the oxygen bottles. "If the war was over, I'd quit today and go back to Texas."

It was till the war was over and they went back to Texas that the workers on the line counted the days, and it was till the quitting whistle at one o'clock that they counted the minutes and the hours. They divided the time at work into four two-hour periods: "till smoke-time" at 6:30, "till lunch" at 8:30, "till smoke-time" again at 11, and "till quitting time" at 1. Time was kept in the ships on the line, not by the standard 24 hours, but by these four whistles; and when, before lunch, someone looked at his watch and said, "Twenty till," he didn't mean twenty minutes to 8 but twenty minutes to lunch at 8:30.

C.M. and I did not wear watches to work. We tried not to look at the clocks on the time card racks in the center aisle, or to ask people around us what time it was, or even to *wonder* what time it was—because during our first week in the plant we had learned one lesson:

It Was Never Later Than We Thought.

Even when we didn't watch the clocks or ask the time, we knew it fairly accurately by the amount of work we had completed, by the actions of the other people in the ship who knew what time it was, and finally by the breathless silence down the line just before a whistle blew.

There were two kinds of time in the plant: "our time" and "company time." We learned to make the distinction even during our first week. "Our time" was the thirty minutes for lunch and the ten minutes for each of the two rest periods, and it was zealously protected by us. "Company time" was the remaining seven hours and forty minutes between 4:30 and 1, and it was jealously guarded for the company by timekeepers, foremen, and leadmen.

The timekeepers, theoretically, were supposed to check four times during the eight hours to see that we were actually on the job. Practically, with several hundred workers to cover, our timekeepers saw us once or possibly twice during an evening. They went around the line, looking up into the ships and recognizing the members of their department by their clothes, their backs, or even their feet. They learned our names, and our numbers, with flattering speed, much more quickly than we learned theirs, for our head timekeeper was constantly bringing some new person up into the ship and introducing him as "your new timekeeper."

The foremen ("Red Buttons," everybody called them, usually prefixing the term with "Damn") kept a protective eye on "company time," peering up into the tail or down through the nose of the ship for loafers. It was our opinion, however, that anyone a foreman could catch loafing would be a poor slow-witted thing who ought to be fired as much for being caught as for loafing, because even the most experienced loafers were always ready with an open tool box so that they could look as if they were working when the slick head of a Red Button appeared below the hatch.

The leadmen were sensitive about loafing on "company time," for the company seemed to be run on the principle that if a worker weren't busy, he should look busy. The leadmen, however, realized that often there was not time to start a new job before the whistle blew — even if there were still five minutes. If someone turned up at the bench with his tool box locked, the leadman would say, "How about hiding out until one o'clock? The boss might be by." Or if the leadman climbed into a ship a few minutes before the final whistle and found a group of girls straightening up their tool boxes, he would say, "This party wouldn't look so good if a Damn Red Button stuck his head in."

The nightly battle for the minutes between the red buttons and the green ones always made us think of that ticking slide film we had seen the first night, "The Power of a Minute." When we remembered that these were the minutes that made the man-hours that built the bombers that would bomb Berlin and Tokyo, there was a murderous power in each minute people waited, "hiding" up in the ships with their hands washed and their tools put away so that they would be "ready" when the whistle blew.

The time spent in getting "ready" for the whistle, going to the rest room and washing up on "company time" varied with the different whistles: least before the rest periods, more before lunch, and most before the quitting whistle. On Saturday night, which had the riotous relief of a Friday at school, some people let out a whoop and laid off when the midnight whistle blew. It was the often-voiced opinion of these people that the company ought to let everyone off at midnight on Saturday — and sometimes I thought the company might as well.

Each of the two rest periods, "smoke-times" as everybody called them, had an individual flavor. The first came at 6:30 during the best part of the day when it was already cool but still sunny. C.M. and I always took a sandwich from our lunch for 6:30 "smokin" because 6:30 still seemed to us like a logical time for food. We ate our sandwiches outside by the field where we could watch the finished Liberators warm up. From the first, we looked at them critically and proudly, much as a mother would look at her children.

Eleven o'clock "smokin" was entirely different from 6:30. By that time people were worn out. They sat silently along the center aisle under the signs that said "Rest Period Smoking Area" or perched on the ladders that led up into the noses of the ships. They looked curiously at C.M. and me because we paraded energetically up and down the aisle on a vain search for the drinking fountains. The location of the drinking fountains was a mystery that had to be solved anew each night, for the center aisle with its line of offices, tool cribs, time clocks, and rest rooms looked very much the same to us no matter where we were. C.M. declared that she personally thought that the foremen hid the drinking fountains; it would be just like them, she said. And one night we actually did see Mr. Billings with a firm grip on one. Of course, he

They sat silently along the center aisle . . .

tried to look as if he were only getting a drink when he saw us.

The rest periods were fun, like the recesses in grammar school; but our favorite time was lunch, not only because it was lunch, but because it was also the time when the line was moved.

The first night when we entered the building, we noticed that the hands on the big clock over Mr. Plunkett's office were at 8 :30 although it was only 6 :30 at the time. His secretary explained to us that the clock was supposed to indicate not the time of day, but the next time the production line was to move. Later the first night when everybody was cautioning us to observe the numbers above the ships so that we wouldn't lose ourselves, somebody told us that before we went to lunch we should notice the numbers on the tail of the ship we were working in.

"Because," he said mysteriously, "at 8 :30 the line will move."

Moving the line sounded quite thrilling to us, although we didn't quite see how anybody was going to move those *big bombers,* encumbered as they were with ladders and platforms and scaffoldings — unless the Lilliputians themselves swarmed out to push and tug the Gullivers along.

"I thought the line was going to move at 8 :30," C.M. said sceptically, biting into an egg sandwich and looking suspiciously at the sleeping monsters, who apparently had no intention of ever moving — let alone flying. Even as she said it, we realized that the great things, ladders, platforms, scaffoldings and all, were actually moving, majestically if creakingly. It was eerie—those monstrous creatures, groaning up from some primordial sleep into slow moving life. It was something for Walt Disney to do as he did Stravinsky's "Rites of Spring."

One night we went down to the U-end of the line to see what happened when the ships moved outside, "around the corner," and up the other line. It was very disillusioning, for two quite mechanical little trucks that didn't look like anything but trucks came out and pulled them around the tracks. After that we ate our lunch back at Station 20 and tried to forget about the little trucks as we watched the ships move.

Lunch, even though it was at 8 :30 in the evening, was "noon" to us. The four hours that came before were "the morning" and the four that came after "the afternoon."

"I did three ships this morning," someone would tell us at lunch-time.

The four hours after lunch were undoubtedly longer than the four before, but we found that they went more quickly if we worked hard and fast to complete an extra job or an extra ship before the final whistle. That was a secret I learned the first week from Sparky. It was nearly 12 :30 when Sparky climbed into the ship with a cheerful "Need some help ?" and proceeded to help. He worked with such speed and concentration that I thought maybe it wasn't really 12 :30, speed and concentration being exceedingly rare at that time of night.

The perspiration was dripping from his face when I thanked him.

"Gee, you're really *fast !*" I marvelled.

He mopped his brow. Then he spat, slowly and deliberately — while my stomach rose, turned over, and fell in the same rhythm. (I remember it distinctly, because it was the first time I had seen a man spit like that. It was not the last.)

"You'll find that time goes faster on this job if you go faster," he told me seriously. "You can loaf if you want to. Nobody will stop you or fire you, and a lot of them won't think any less of you. It's just a matter of what you think of yourself. You feel better when you work for your money."

But no matter how hard and fast we tried to work, the hour after midnight went slowly. We couldn't help hearing people say, "Thirty-five more minutes," "Just half an hour," "Only twenty-five," "Twenty more," "Fifteen more," "Ten," "Five," "*Only a minute !*" Then they waited in breathless silence for the whistle that would bring them closer by another day to the end of the war and Texas again.

At one o'clock, it blew.

CHAPTER EIGHT

ONCE C.M. got out a pencil and paper and we tried to figure out where they went, those twenty-four hours that were supposed to be in every day. It made us feel better to put them down on paper so we could see that a couple *weren't* being deducted the way dollars were deducted from our checks.

From 4:30 to 1 we were at work. That was eight and a half hours. It took us an hour to get home. Nine and a half. An hour to get ready for bed, what with putting up hair and washing out things. Ten and a half. A half hour to read — papers, mail, and books. Eleven. Seven and a half hours of sleep, because for the summer we had conceded a half hour of our usual eight as a time-saving measure. That was eighteen and a half. A half hour for breakfast and an hour to clean ourselves up. (An hour was *not* a generous allowance.) Twenty. Then it took us an hour to get dinner and put up lunches and dress for work — and another hour to get to work. Twenty-two hours. That left us exactly two hours, one hundred and twenty minutes, in which to write, to draw, and to acquire the tan that makes summer really summer. Our main trouble seemed to be that we were trying to build bombers, write a book, and have a vacation all at the same time. One of the three had to go. We had agreed to build the bombers, we wanted to write the book — and so the vacation went.

The best thing about the whole affair was that "on

nights" we were richer than we would have been "on days," for we made more and we spent less. We didn't have time to spend money—just time to sleep to work, to eat to work, to wash to work, and *to work*. Sometimes we tried to save time, to gain extra minutes by complicated schedules and short-cuts; but these always left unscheduled time-consuming things like letters to Fred, telephone conversations with our friends, and trips to the corner grocery. They also involved skimping on the time we had allowed for sleeping and eating, since we could *not* skimp on the time allowed for washing and working.

One week we got up at 10 instead of 11. That was wonderful, although it took an *alarm clock* to do it and an alarm clock sounded ridiculously out of place at 10 in the morning. We congratulated ourselves—one whole hour to the good. But the fifth day we simply collapsed and slept right around the clock until three in the afternoon—and there went all the hours we had saved. Sleep it seemed was unfortunately a "must"—unfortunately because although we were always tired, we were never sleepy except when we had to get up in the morning. Yet if we lost our sleep, we lost our complexions, our dispositions, and our energy. Instead of being attractively languid, we were crabby; and our eyes, instead of having glamorous circles under them, were bloodshot. Seven and a half hours' sleep was evidently our irreducible minimum, although during our first two weeks on the job we did find that we woke up, without an alarm, after only six hours of sleep. In no time, however, our sleeping habits adjusted themselves to the new schedule that ran into the sunlight hours of the morning and we were sleeping our regular seven and a half hours again.

During the first two weeks we also found that we slept *hard*. When we woke up in the morning, we had the tired stiff feeling of having slept in exactly the same position all night. We had great scars where the wrinkles in the sheet had dug into our flesh, every bone was stiff and aching, and our hands had to be opened and closed to see if they were still in operating order. When we fell into bed at night, and we did *fall* in, we always selected our spot and position with great care because we knew that we would be in that exact spot and position until morning.

Once we tried to save time by giving up breakfast and gaining the half hour we had allowed for it. That was fine, one whole half hour to the good, but our stomachs growled with hunger all the rest of the morning and we gave up the experiment in despair. Eating was also unfortunately a "must"—unfortunately because although we were always hungry, we never had any appetite for our food. To say that loss of appetite was unusual for us is an understatement. Gluttony has always been our private Deadly Sin. We love breakfast. We love lunch. We love dinner. We especially love the things that come in-between, "piecing," my mother calls it, and "spoiling your dinner." On the Swing Shift, however, the *only* meal that interested us even slightly came out of our lunch boxes at 8:30. It was hard to be enthusiastic about food when we had to eat breakfast, prepare lunch, and eat dinner all within the space of four hours. Still we were mightily disturbed. Here were we, who had always lived to eat, eating to live. Everybody who knew us was disturbed. My mother fluttered over us and tempted us with small breakfast delicacies. C.M.'s Pops created his most wonderful garlicky dishes and set them before us. Fred, disturbed too, wrote for god's sake, were we sick? We wrote back that we weren't sick; we simply were *not* interested in food, except after work at one o'clock when we thought longingly of coffee and doughnuts or gooey concoctions topped with whipped cream, nuts, and cherries. But we had taken a solemn vow at the beginning

62

of the summer that we would never, absolutely never, under any conditions, not even as a special celebration on pay nights, take *one* small bite after work. We had heard that people who work at night often gain weight because they eat four meals a day (one after work) instead of three. We thought bitterly that it would be *too much* to work on the production line all summer and get fat *besides!*

C.M. inquired among the other workers in the bomb bay to find out what they did about their meals. One man said that he ate a light breakfast when he got up, then dinner just before he came to work in the middle of the afternoon, and lunch at the plant. A girl said that she and her husband, who also worked on the Swing Shift, ate breakfast right before they came to work, then lunch at the plant, and dinner when they got home at two o'clock in the morning. Another girl said that she ate peanuts all night at work, *five* bags of them, with a quart of milk at lunch. Then she had a *big* dinner after work. (This menu always upset us just a little.) Before work we saw all three of these people at the Aircraft Café or Tony's ice cream wagon or the little mobile commissaries inside, buying soft drinks or coffee and munching popcorn or candy. The truth of the matter was that most people on the Swing Shift ate *all* the time. They ate during both rest periods as well as at lunch-time, and they ate when they arrived at work and when they got off. They ate between meals because they had no appetite at meal-time, and they had no appetite at meal-time because they ate between meals. It was one of those trite but still vicious circles that people talk about.

Another vicious circle was trying to get the grease out of our clothes, the metal dust out of our hair, and the dirt out of our nails so that we could go to work and get more grease on our clothes, more metal dust in our hair, and more dirt under our nails. We were clean. We were dirty. We were clean. We were dirty. Only mostly we were dirty. Our problem was not keeping clean, but getting clean — once a day to prove that we could do it. Getting clean was an ordeal. It started at one o'clock at the circular fountain by the time clock. There we took off our jackets and scrubbed our hands and arms up to the sleeves of our T-shirts with the powerful powdered soap in the containers at the center of the fountain.

This nightly ritual affected C.M. strangely. One night she announced brightly that it made her feel like Lady Macbeth.

"Lady Macbeth?" said the man who was washing up next to us. "What's Lady Macbeth got to do with *this*?"

"'Out, damned spot! Out, I say!'" quoted C.M. as she vigorously rubbed soap into her knuckles. "'All the perfumes of Araby will not sweeten this little hand.'"

"Huh!" said the man, looking curiously at her. He always looked curiously at her after that. "Lady Macbeth, huh!" he would mutter.

The session at the fountain by the time clock was only the beginning. There we tried to get the worst dirt off with the company soap and water, what with the soap and water shortage in San Diego. The real session was in the bathtub at home, where we lathered and scrubbed and dug into the corners for dirt, admired the color of the washcloth and the bath water and the ring around the tub. C.M. and I are the kind of people who get an esthetic pleasure out of cleaning something really dirty — and really dirty was what we were. In a place where a person could get dirty by simply sitting and letting the dust fall on him, we were distinguished by the grime on our hands, the grease on our arms, and the dust on our clothes. True enough, Mrs. Hires at the Employment Office had made a great point of the fact that we would get our hands dirty; she had *not* told us that we would get dirt in our hair, in our ears and our noses, down our necks, between our toes (We don't know *how* either!), and all over our clothes. Our blue slacks were so dusty that when we put on the jacket that went with them, someone always said tactlessly, "You have the wrong jacket, don't you? That one isn't the same color the pants are." "Under the grey, the blue"—that described our uniforms. We were comforted, however, by Mr. Billings' pronouncement, made one night as we were washing up at the fountain.

"A foreman can always tell how hard a girl works," said Mr. Billings, our foreman, "by how dirty she gets."

"Mr. Billings," said C.M. aside to me, "must have a very high opinion of us!"

Before the 4:30 whistle blew, C.M. and I always smeared a protective cream over our hands and arms, rubbing it into our elbows and knuckles and under our nails. This stuff, which smelled like soap and felt like cream and was probably a combination of the two, was supposed to keep the dirt from penetrating the pores—it said on the jar. The only trouble was that while it kept us cleaner it made us look dirtier, or, as C.M. said technically, the dirt came off more easily but there was more of it.

Since we were living on a very economical summer budget, of which the cream was a major item of expense, we never washed at work, except very daintily at our finger tips, because if we did we would have to apply more cream. This saving habit of ours caused some difficulty when we went to First Aid to be treated for our various injuries received in the line of duty.

"Wash your hands," the white-starched nurse would say disdainfully before she would sprinkle a powdered sulfa drug from a little metal salt shaker, on the injury.

We would carefully scrub the area around the injury, but nowhere else, and offer our hands again.

"I said to wash your hands," the nurse would say imperatively ; or if it were still early in the evening when we weren't really dirty yet, she would say scornfully, "You didn't do a very good job, did you?"

We would point out carefully that we had washed *around* the injury, and we would explain that we couldn't afford to wash the entire hand because then we would have to apply more cream. Our trips to First Aid were so frequent that soon we became known to the slightly bewildered nurse as "the girls who don't wash their hands."

One night we were in First Aid when the nurse was giving soap-and-water advice to a girl who had developed a collection of pimples since she had come to work in the plant. We impressed the nurse then by announcing that *we* scrubbed our faces with soap and water *three* times a day — because we didn't want her to think that we *never* washed our hands.

That was the Swing Shift for you! Sleep. Eat. Work. Wash. Sleep. Eat. Work. Wash. We quite frankly hated it until one day — One day we met a friend on the street.

"*My!*" she said, looking us over admiringly. "What have you two been doing to yourselves?"

She looked at our figures, which were pounds lighter and inches thinner. She looked at our complexions, which were clearer and smoother. Then she looked at our tans, which we had eked out on a short but regular daily sunbath.

"*My!*" she said enviously. "What are you doing this summer? You must be having a wonderful time!"

CHAPTER NINE

IT was bad enough being tired all the time and dirty most of the time, but worst of all the first week was having to go to work in slacks—down Fourth Street where people who knew us acted as if they didn't, or down Third Street where people who didn't know us whistled as if they did.

In war-time San Diego there are just two kinds of women: the ones who go to work in skirts and the ones who go in slacks. The girls who work in slacks are sometimes cleaner and neater than the girls who work in skirts. They usually make more money than their skirted sisters behind the ribbon counter at the Five and Ten or at the controls of the elevator in the bank. *But* they have to wear slacks. Whether they are dust-bowl mothers buying butter and eggs for the first time, or former dime store clerks making more money than army majors, or war wives who feel they must keep them flying because their husbands are flying them, or school teachers putting in a summer vacation on a war job, they are women who work in slacks instead of skirts.

If you don't think there's a difference, just put on a Consolidated uniform and try to get service in your favorite store, make a reservation at a ticket office, or get information at the post office. Either the clerks have no conception of the position of a customer in a buying and selling economy—or they don't consider aircraft workers customers. Our prize example of such a clerk was the girl behind the counter at the café outside Gate Two, where delectable Double Decker Chocolate Ice Cream Cones were sold every afternoon. The first time we took our money up to the crowded counter, we were terrified by this clerk.

"Whaddayawant?" she snarled out of the edges of her mouth to the people ahead of us, who naturally wanted Double Decker Chocolate Ice Cream Cones too. "Shut up and wait your turn. I'll get to you when I'm good and ready!"

We melted away the first time before the wrath of this creature, who ironically bore the name of Bonnie embroidered on the sleeve of her dirty uniform. The second time we had to wait so long at the counter that we finally returned the quarter we had borrowed for the purchase and went into the plant. And the third time——! The third time we made a special effort to get to the counter in plenty of time. We even brought our own quarter with us that day. I held it up conspicuously for twenty-five minutes while Bonnie scooped up wonderful, drooly cones, four at a time, for the people ahead of us. The last one before she got to us was a special achievement, almost a triple-decker because it had an extra gob on top.

"Well, whaddayawant?" Bonnie growled as we drooled gently.

C.M. said we would like *two* Double Decker Chocolate Ice Cream Cones, please. The "please" she added hopefully. I held up the quarter.

"No more chocolate ice cream," Bonnie said shortly to us and to the man next to us, "Whaddayawant?" We turned away sadly.

We never did get Double Decker Chocolate Ice Cream Cones, not all summer. I think we were the only people who went through Gate Two who never went through

68

licking beautiful spirals around Double Decker Chocolate Ice Cream Cones.

It was bad enough to have clerks ignore us, to have the members of our own sex scorn us; but what really hurt was the attitude of men. In one way, we were not women at all as far as they were concerned — if having them give us their seats on a crowded bus or stand aside to let us pass or pick up something we dropped meant that we were women. In another way, we were definitely women to them — "skirts" is the old-fashioned term, although it isn't appropriate today. Men lounging on corners looked us over in a way we didn't like, from head to toe with special focus on the "empennage" (a term for the tail assembly of an airplane with obvious implications as a slang word applied to the female form). Men grabbed us and followed us and whistled at us. They called us "Sister" in a most unbrotherly way and "Baby" in a most unfatherly way.

It was a great shock to C.M. and me to find that being a lady depended more upon our clothes than upon ourselves. We had always gone on the theory that the only girls men tried to pick up were the ones who looked as if they could be picked up. Armed in our dignified school-teacher-hood and our glasses, we were content to go unmolested with only a reassuring whistle now and then from a truck driver or a soldier in a jeep. This summer we found out that it was not our innate dignity that protected us from unwelcome attentions, but our trim suits, big hats, white gloves, and spectator pumps. Clothes, we reflected sadly, make the woman — and some clothes make the man think that he can make the woman. In our dusty blue slacks we were "Sister" and "Baby;" and even our glasses, Dorothy Parker to the contrary notwithstanding, were no protection.

Thus it was something of a problem to get home at two o'clock in the morning. Before he left, Fred had given us a short course in jiujitsu, instructed us not to speak to strangers or accept candy and rides from them, and told us to practice diligently on the living room floor the three throws he had shown us. Under strict orders from Fred, we were to alternate between Clara Marie's "attic" downtown and my house on the Point so that we could protect each other.

If we went home to the attic, we faced the problem of the servicemen who wanted to carry our lunch boxes, help us up the hill, or show us the town. One night three sailors bore down on us, swept off their caps, bowed gravely, and said in unison, "We salute you, Ladies of the Production Line, and we thank you !" We walked coolly past them, looking straight ahead—although I told C.M. later that if we had been the girls in "The Human Comedy" we would have returned the salute and the thanks with a kiss for each of them right there on the corner. C.M. snorted that such things were all right for William Saroyan ; he wasn't under *strict orders* from Fred.

C.M. always handled such difficult situations for us because I usually began to laugh. One night, for instance, we were climbing the hill to the attic, so dusty and tired that even our lunch boxes weighed on us like Pilgrim's burden, when two marines started to follow us, calling, "Let me carry your dinner bucket, Baby !" and "How about a little war work, Sister ?" We ignored them and walked faster. They ignored our ignoring them and walked faster. We walked faster. They walked faster— until they caught up with us, one on each side. One slipped his arm through C.M.'s and the other slipped his through mine. *Now,* I thought, was the time for the jiujitsu. I mentally rehearsed the three throws Fred had taught us, but they all started from a position in which

I was flat on my back on the living room floor. At this point C.M. came to the rescue.

She stopped so suddenly that the marine who was holding her arm was swung around in front of her.

"Sir!" she said, stamping her foot and speaking in her best classroom voice—although it did quaver a little. "Will you please stop following us *this instant*? We have been working hard all night. We're tired and we don't want to be bothered. Now go away and leave us alone," she finished petulantly.

With this she turned on her heel, and I trailed in admiration. The two marines received her oration like the Gettysburg Address, with perfect silence. When I sneaked a look back at the next corner, they were still standing there looking after us.

We did not rate such attention from the United States Army, Navy, and Marine Corps, however, when we went home to my house on the Point Loma bus. The Point Loma bus ran from the downtown plaza to Fort Rosecrans, past the civic center, the tuna factory, three aircraft plants, the marine base, the naval training station, the Portuguese settlement, and two residential districts. This route gave it a cosmopolitan passenger list, which included us at two o'clock in the morning.

When the Point Loma bus stopped (if it stopped at all) at Gate Two, it was usually so crowded that getting us in was like putting something you have forgotten into a weekend bag. After we squeezed ourselves in, sailors, soldiers, and marines returning from an evening in town looked up at us sleepily or drunkenly— we couldn't tell the difference. C.M. said charitably that maybe the reason they didn't offer us their seats was that they couldn't stand up, not that they wouldn't. The truth was though that the two women in skirts who got on at the same time we did were always offered seats. One was a company nurse, all in spotless white which she tried to keep as far as possible from our dusty blue — and that wasn't very far on the Point Loma bus. She always got a seat, but that may have been a tribute to her profession and not to the fact that she wore a skirt. The other woman was an office worker. She squeaked like a talking doll and she chewed gum in a way that in the classroom would have me saying, "Put your gum in the basket, Mary." C.M. and I looked askance at her, but that was nothing to the way she looked at us. *She* always got a seat ; and since it could not be because she was lady-like, beautiful, or intelligent, we decided it must be because she wore a skirt.

We didn't begrudge the nurse and the office worker their seats — very much ! After all, they had been working for eight hours too. What really hurt was the fact that when girls got on with their dates after what had obviously been an evening of merry making at the local dance hall, half a dozen men would spring to their feet and offer them their seats !

We and the other women in slacks stood while the bus deposited two loads of marines and four loads of sailors at their respective gates. Each of these stops was a complicated procedure involving the solicitous prodding of an unconscious serviceman by a nearby buddy who would ask three or four times before he got an answer, "Where do you get off, Mac ?" Mac (the name common to all servicemen) usually muttered something that sounded vaguely like "Gate Ten" (which was non-existent) or "Right here" (which must have been a wild guess because he never looked up to see where he was). Mac was then led up the aisle, oozing gently over the other passengers. The obliging buddy, who had evidently never seen him before, collected his cap and paid his fare. If we were quick, we could get Mac's deserted seat before some man got it — but usually we were not that quick. The man who did get the seat sometimes took pity on us and chivalrously offered to hold us on his lap.   We always answered this offer with our

C.M. said maybe they *couldn't* stand up . . .

haughtiest stare, which was much more effective when we were in skirts than when we were in slacks with dusty circles on the knees and the seat of the pants.

Our *greatest scorn* we saved for the officers who sat comfortably in front of us and looked glassily right through us. We reflected bitterly to ourselves that even an Act of Congress hadn't made gentlemen out of them.

"Some day," C.M. threatened, "when one of them stands up to get off, I'm going to say, 'Oh, thank you *so much !*', and sit down."

I suggested that if we ever did get a seat, we should get up and offer it to an ensign. (We particularly disliked the ensigns because there were so many of them sitting down.) C.M. said nothing doing ; if she *ever* got a seat on the Point Loma bus, she was going to sit in it herself.

On our first Sunday off, just to reassure ourselves that it was the slacks and not us, we put on our bright linen suits, our highest heels, our whitest gloves, and our biggest hats and went for a ride on the Point Loma bus. And when three sailors, two marines, a soldier, and even *two* ensigns rose to offer us their seats, we said "Thank you !" as if we were used to such attention — and we took the ensigns' seats !

CHAPTER TEN

PEOPLE on the outside were always impressed when C.M. told them that *she* strung the electric wires that made the bombs drop. When I added eagerly that I put in the safety belt holders, the safety straps, the compass brackets, the cable pulleys, and the sens-antenna straps *too,* they were not impressed. They merely smiled indulgently — as if they thought that Consolidated had exhibited remarkable ingenuity in finding a few small tasks simple enough for me to perform. The only way that I could get any attention at all was to drop into the conversation the fact that I worked in "the tunnel."

"The tunnel?" they asked, abruptly interrupting C.M.'s elaborate description of the bomb bay. They all knew what the bomb bay was, but the tunnel? "What's that?" they asked.

I explained that the tunnel was what we who worked there called the tail section of the ship, for a tunnel was exactly what it looked like with its long arched ceiling that stretched from the tail gunner's turret to the place where the wings joined inside the ship. Having wrested the conversational ball from C.M. (no mean trick in itself), I always hung onto it and explained in detail what working in the tunnel was like — just as I am going to do right now while she sits silent until the next chapter when she can tell you about the bomb bay.

At the nose end of the tunnel, a foot or so below the ceiling, was the curving riveted surface of the wings.

This spot was always nearer to the center of the ship than I ever expected it to be, so that during my early days on the line I was always confused about which end was which. Before I climbed into a ship, I used to look at it thoughtfully and *decide* which end was the nose and which the tail. Once inside, I always lost all sense of direction; having entered from the rear, I persisted in referring to everything toward the nose as "the back" and everything toward the tail as "the front." The other people working in the tunnel would look at me bewilderedly then and say, "Pardon how ?" Most of them referred to the nose end as "fore" and the tail end as "aft."

Work in the tunnel was usually carried on to the accompaniment of vocal selections from a man and a woman who worked flat on their backs on the surface of the wings to the fore. The woman never knew the same words that the man did, but they harmonized pleasantly if a trifle whiskily on all the old favorites. They practiced diligently for a future appearance on one of the local amateur shows, but always stopped singing when someone else joined in on the chorus. I privately thought that it would be very inspiring to have all the workers in the tunnel singing "God Bless America" as they worked — just like in the movies; but evidently they didn't.

The wings entered the ship right in front of the command deck, a hands-and-knees sort of place above the bomb bay. The command deck was not what I would call spacious even to begin with when the tail section came in at Station 1 from the Parts Plant, its walls not yet encumbered with tubes, wires, cables, brackets, and oxygen bottles. By the time a ship reached Station 20, its command deck contained not only an assortment of awkward tables, brackets, and boxes for radio equipment, but also half a dozen oxygen bottles the size and shape of *big* watermelons. It was amazing how many people could still wedge in among these objects, packing themselves in with cardboard, blankets, and pillows to protect their knees from the washboard-like aluminum floor of the command deck.

The people who worked there were usually from Department 140- Radio or 100- Inspection, but the group always included one man who held a bucking bar for a riveter out on the wing. A bucking bar is a heavy metal piece which provides a solid backing for the rivet, and this man always had spread out on the radio table the two dozen different ones he needed for the intricacies of this particular job. Each bar was of a particular size and shape to fit into a particular corner where a rivet had to go. The man who held the bucking bar was always large and long, and he filled in all the space that was left on one side of the command deck after the radio equipment had been installed. The people from 140 and 100 acted as if he were simply part of the floor and worked on top of him. I wondered if this attitude would not leave his personality, as well as his physique, somewhat crushed.

In addition to these permanent residents of the command deck, there was a steady procession of transients who popped in for one small job and then out again. One of these was the tubby grey-haired woman known on the line as "Grandma" because she was constantly bragging about her grandson's promotions in the army. Every night Grandma climbed with difficulty up through the hatch, stepped over and around everybody working in the main section of the tunnel, managed her way precariously around the belly turret, crawled up onto the command deck, and tucked herself into a small awkward corner. There she held a bucking bar while someone in the bomb bay rattled in *one* rivet. Then she squeezed herself out of the corner, panted "Pardon me" to the people on the command deck, made another dangerous journey around the belly turret, pushed through the people and the equipment in the main section of the tunnel, and, her job completed, disappeared down the ladder.

The section right behind the command deck was reserved for the belly gun turret, a handsome ball which we were informed was worth five thousand dollars all by itself. The belly turret was a recent innovation when C.M. and I first started to work on the line; and remembering our sworn statement that we had read the Espionage Act, Executive Order of the President of the United States, No. 8381, we considered it our personal responsibility to President Roosevelt to keep its existence secret from the general public. We firmly repressed *every* temptation to impress our relatives and friends with our knowledge of it. Then one day we got one of our rare glances at a morning paper, and there in a two column picture on the *front page,* accompanied by an article giving more facts than anyone on the line knew, was the *secret* belly turret!

The belly turret was always a favorite of mine, for it had the round placid look of Tik Tok of Oz. I observed the complicated process of its installation in the tunnel with interest. When a ship moved down the line into Department 192, the great hole left in the floor of the tunnel for the turret was covered so that we could walk across it to the command deck; but as soon as a ship entered 192, a little man zipped into the tunnel, removed the boards, and fitted a large jig into the space so that he would know where to drill the holes for the turret. Like Truth at the bottom of a well, he stood calmly down in the hole where the turret would later hang, serenely drilling his holes, apparently unaware of the danger he was in as people like me, loaded down with *heavy* equipment, stepped around or over the space in which he was working. I say that he was apparently unaware of his danger, but I noticed that when he did look up through his cage-like jig at me, he looked as if he were praying. Probably he had heard of the assistant foreman's narrow escape from my electric motor.

After the little man removed his jig, the two lads who installed the turret itself arrived in the tunnel. They ignored the rest of us and talked together in a strange language of their own creation which consisted of using goddamn as a prefix for the name of every tool they used and sonuvabitch for the name of every person they spoke of. They never smiled as they carefully raised and lowered the turret into position. Later in the summer they both achieved a certain notoriety on the line when a zoot-suiter stabbed one in the back during a dance hall brawl and two girls staged a fist fight over the other during lunch-time. (I could understand the action of the zoot-suiter, but not that of the girls.)

After they installed the turret, they covered it with a bright red wood igloo which bore the pidgin English warning "No Step!" on the top. The warning was a little difficult to read, because it was usually under somebody's foot.

The pleasantest part of the tunnel to work in was the section between the belly turret and the hatch; it was the widest and highest and it also had a large hatch on either side, where the waist-gunners would later stand. Besides increasing the ventilation, these hatches offered fine opportunities for observing the approach of a friend — or a Red Button.

The main disadvantage of working in this section of the tunnel was the floor — although calling it a floor does not give exactly the right impression. The actual floor of the tunnel, like the floor of the command deck, was simply a huge washboard. On the line, however, it was covered (I don't know whether it was to protect the washboard from our feet, or our knees from the washboard) with a set of thin red floorboards which were supposed to fit together like the pieces of a jigsaw puzzle. Of course, they never were fitted together; and there were always more floorboards than there was space for them to cover. We women rarely straightened them out, preferring rather to balance our stools precariously upon them; but the men, when they climbed into the tunnel, disgustedly heaved the

The pleasantest place was in front of the hatch.

extra boards out the side hatch and onto the platform of the next ship and cleared out the various things which were under the remaining floorboards. They always accompanied this "housekeeping" (That's what it was called on the line!) with a brief dissertation on why women are mentally, physically, and morally unsuited to be factory workers. The men always seemed to be more conscious of safety hazards than the women — or maybe they were naturally tidier.

Whenever the floor of the tunnel was piled highest with extra floorboards, motors, stools, tool boxes, tubes, cables, parts, and paper bags of bolts and nuts, all of which were hopelessly tangled in electric cords, then one of two people always arrived : either the sad man who had to move all the paraphernalia, rip up the floorboards, and lift the center wedge-shaped section of the washboard floor to check the hydraulic installations for the tail skid ; or (and I was never able to decide which one was the more unwelcome) the cheery man who threw a dozen or so yellow-green oxygen bottles up into the tunnel and then hung them in the felt-lined hoop-like straps above our heads.

Sam, who checked the hydraulic installations, had been graduated from college in the very early thirties and had been passed from one white collar job to another at $16 a week for enough years to make him happily cynical now that his weekly pay-check grossed in the eighties. His wife also worked at Consolidated in the engineering department.

"We're really socking it away," Sam told me. "No more depressions for us !"

Joe, who installed the oxygen bottles, had not been graduated from college ; in fact, he had not been graduated from high school. He had left the eighth grade some twenty-five years ago to follow the booms from state to state. He said it had been fun. Joe was never serious except when he was explaining to me that we were really building bombers for the Chase National Bank and not for the government, or telling me that he considered Lindbergh more of a Paul Revere than a Benedict Arnold. The rest of the time he was inveigling someone into playing "Catch the Bottle" with him so that he wouldn't have to climb up into the tunnel with each one, or he was offering some philosophical comfort, usually culled from the motion pictures, which he attended regularly in the early morning after work.

"All the world's a stage," he told me one night, "and all the men and women merely players on it. Al Jolson said that," he added.

"I thought Shakespeare said it," I murmured.

"Well, maybe Shakespeare said it too," he conceded graciously.

Joe always sang "As Time Goes By" while he strapped in the bottles. He thought it was the greatest song ever written—lots of philosophy in it, he told me. Besides the fact that the presence of a dozen oxygen bottles was conspicuous, I could always tell when Joe had been in a ship because somebody would be singing, "You must remember this . . ."

The narrow section of the tunnel which lay between the hatch and the tail gunner's turret looked even more like a tunnel than the rest of the tail section, for it was much narrower. At the very end was a large metal bowl in which the turret would be installed farther down the line. The man who installed the rejector chutes for the used ammunition occupied this bowl, and he always looked as if he were taking a bath in an old-fashioned tub.

That was the tunnel—and it was surprising how soon it came to look more familiar to me than my own room at school. I could even say, "I left it on the command deck," as calmly as I used to say, "It's in the bottom left hand drawer." All night—every night—I went from ship to ship, climbing up the ladder into the tail to make my installations and climbing down again. A great many other people did the same thing. The result was that at the last station on the line, the walls of the tunnel, which had been blank and bare at the first station, were covered with tubes, wires and brackets, ready for action!

CHAPTER ELEVEN

THE fact that we were building bombers seemed a dubious contribution to the war effort to the people who knew about it. My mother said it was unfortunate that our fliers had to contend with us as well as with the Japs and the Germans, and C. M.'s Pops asked with concern if our work were checked by someone else before the ships went into the air. Fred just wrote for god's sake to be careful! The general fear seemed to be that I would put in safety belt holders that wouldn't hold and that C.M. would cross the wires in the bomb bay so that at the crucial moment the ship would drop instead of the bombs. C.M. said that of course such an idea was perfectly ridiculous, that Pappy said she was "catching on" remarkably well and that she would be "all right."

"Pappy says," C.M. began, with the reverence she usually reserves for Fred's pronouncements, "Pappy says that 85 per cent of the work on an airplane can be done by unskilled labor." (This was a comforting thought, since at least 85 per cent of it was being done by unskilled labor.)

Pappy was the chief of the electrical crew to which Mr. Tompkinson ("Ned" to the people under him, who were very surprised to learn from C.M. that his last name was Tompkinson) had assigned her the first night. C.M. referred to Pappy as her "mentor" and he was well qualified for the job, for he had "mentored" the first girl electricians on the B-24 line a year and a half before. The only thing the girls hadn't been taught at the training school was how to solder, and that was what they had been hired to do ; but I bet Pappy taught them to solder, and to solder well, all the while addressing them as "Daughter," as he did every female on the line.

Pappy "Daughter'd" C.M. and Emeline, the other girl on the crew, and they "Pappy'd" him until the bomb bay sounded like a family circle. At first C.M. supposed that since Pappy addressed Emeline as "daughter," he must be on quite intimate terms with her. She was somewhat surprised, therefore, when she discovered that he didn't even know her name.

Like most middle-aged men on the production line, Pappy had led so unsettled a roving existence — farmer, organ repairer, yachtsman — that he was able in middle life to take up an entirely new vocation in the aircraft industry. He had gone to agricultural college ; and when he told C.M. one night about the slow nine-year failure of his one farming venture (raising prize peaches when prize peaches were selling for $1.50 a ton), she said it was as if she could see what had put the lines in the man's face.

Pappy had the slack, powerful look of a retired blacksmith ; and although he had never been one, he came by the look naturally. His grandmother had actually been the village smithy, having taken up her prospector husband's trade to support her seven little boys when he disappeared into the Mother Lode country during the Gold Rush Days.

"Damn fine blacksmith, too," said Pappy, spitting accurately for the outside corner of the bomb bay. (Spitting took the place of capitals and periods in male conversation on the production line.)

C.M. admired Pappy for his gracious dignity, his thick dark gold hair, which lay in deep waves in back and just peeked over the brow in front, *and* his perfectly marvellous tool chest, out of which he could produce a variety of unusual tools for the other members of the crew which he, individualist that he was, disdained to use. His assorted bolts and nuts, every kind used "in electrical," he kept in a neat row of metal snuff boxes in the top tray of the chest. The last box in the row actually contained snuff, which Pappy had started to take in the early masculine days of the plant when there were no "smoke-times" every two hours. The snuff C.M. and I inspected with curiosity because we had only read about it. It looked like wet chili powder, tasted like salt and red pepper, and had a familiar spicy aroma which we immediately recognized because it was one of the characteristic smells of the production line. When we began to notice, we were surprised at how many round snuff boxes we saw in tool chests and how many times we saw men spread the dark powder along their lower lips.

When the starting whistle blew at 4:30, C.M. and Emeline and Pappy always disappeared into a bomb bay, lugging with them tool boxes, lights, and stools. They stayed in that bomb bay until they had finished the electrical work there and then moved on to another. Farther down the line, a clean-up crew went over their work to correct errors and fill in shortages. A boy on this clean-up crew told Emeline that Pappy's bomb bays required the least clean-up, and there was much rejoicing when she recounted this glad news to Pappy and C.M. The three of them looked with great scorn upon Mr. Tompkinson's other electrical crews. One of these was under Babe, who, with a characteristic female lack of executive ability, had taught each member of her group only a special section of the work so that before a ship was completed Babe herself had to scurry around after all the last odds and ends. Another was under a man known as Peapicker, who had a *system* for doing the bomb bay. In this system, Peapicker drilled all the holes, someone else put up all the clips, Peapicker tightened all the bolts, and someone else held all the nuts. This elaborate division of labor was not approved by Pappy's crew, whose system consisted of each member's beginning at a different corner of the bomb bay and working until he met the others.

Pappy's citadel was the bomb bay, the section in the belly of the ship, the front half below the wings and the back half below the command deck, where the bombs are stored. C.M. was unreasonably proud of working in the bomb bay because she pointed out that the whole ship was hung from the center of the wings above her head, as if the structure which she observed with such respect were something to her own credit. The bomb bay was divided cross-wise by a metal frame and length-wise by a narrow catwalk. At the rear of the bomb bay, so that C.M. did not forget where she was working and why she was stringing wires, were the instructions, which looked like cross-word puzzles, for loading the bomb racks.

Now, much has been written about the Black Hole of Calcutta, but the Black Hole of Calcutta was *NOTHING* compared to the bomb bay, the capitals being C.M.'s To climb into the bomb bay she had to bend down at the same time she stepped up on the platform under the ship ; and if she made the slightest error in judging the distance, she scraped her back on the knife-like edge of the bomb bay doors, which slid down on both sides like a roll-top desk. Even if she did avoid the Back Scraper, once inside the bomb bay, she could hardly expect to dodge the Elbow Catcher too, the Elbow Catcher being a fiendish contraption that had something to do with releasing the bombs. And if by the best of luck she did elude the Elbow Catcher, the Head Bumper was sure to get her, the Head Bumper having been installed under the pretense that it was the jig for the 2000 pound bomb rack. (A jig is to an airplane part what a dressmaker's dummy is to a human figure.)

Working in the bomb bay, according to C.M., was like "carrying-on" during an air raid — if the air raid were

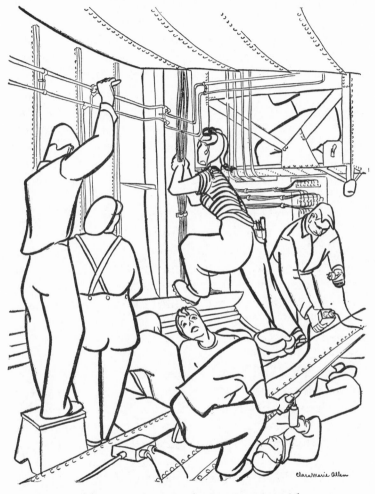

It was like carrying on during an air raid . . .

taking place *inside* a crowded bomb shelter. There were the air raid noises — rattling, screeching, crashing sounds of rivet guns and drills and mallets — and then there were the things that fell from above. Most of the hardships of life in the bomb bay arose from the fact that it was underneath everything and everybody, and being under anything or anybody in an airplane factory is dangerous when you recall that 85 per cent of the labor is unskilled. Working above the bomb bay were people on the flight deck and the command deck and in the life raft compartment above the wings. C.M. soon learned to recognize these people by their legs and their curses. They sent down a steady stream of bolts and nuts, and sometimes they dropped their tools. Then they came springing down into the bomb bay with great speed because unless they were quick their tools would be gone. As Mr. Billings had told us our first night, this was no Sunday school.

The people working outside on the wings couldn't drop things directly into the bomb bay on C.M. so they poked them in from the sides: little tubes of metal, big rubber hose-like things, stiff cables, thin scratchy gold wires, and little black semi-flexible cables whose cool metal ends gently caressed the back of her neck until the goosebumps started to rise and she thought wildly of black water snakes. The people working on the wings probably did not mean to impale C.M. on their various small weapons, but they did not expect to find a human head where hers was. They couldn't see her and they couldn't hear her, so they threw things into the bomb bay with cheerful abandon and she dodged them with all the agility her position on the catwalk permitted. She said she tried singing once as a method of warning, which her singing is, but a handful of dural sifted down from the command deck into her open mouth, and that stopped that.

Usually when the people above the bomb bay started to drill, they sang out, "Dural coming down!" or "Sawdust below!," which meant the same thing as "Fore!" in golf. In theory this was to warn people in the bomb bay to keep their heads down so that they wouldn't get metal dust in their eyes, but what really happened was that C.M. promptly looked up to see what they were saying just as the shining flecks of dural showered down. They sifted through her clothes, even her underwear, and got into her ears and her hair. Sometimes tiny splinters of dural even worked their way into her skin where they raised little red splotches. These little splinters were fondly known as "dural termites" and the splotches as "dural bites," dural being short for duralumin, the light, strong aluminum alloy used in aircraft construction.

Pappy's crew usually spent most of the night in one ship and became quite chummy with the other people who worked in the bomb bay, reaching over them and under them and around them. C.M. found out that a bomber has certain things in common with the house that Jack built, for there was a steady procession of men and women who drilled the holes that held the studs that fastened the covers that protected something or other from the weather. (The B-24's were sieve-like in the rain, and everything that should not get wet had to have a cover. Pappy, who had worked in ships on the field during a storm, told C.M. that surprisingly a bomber was leakier when it was standing still than when it was moving.)

In the crowded bomb bay C.M. moved along her side, working under the man who put in the pipes that ran above her wires and over the woman who ran the control cables under them. She carefully avoided the girl who connected the gay automatic control wires, dodged the man who hammered the pulleys for the control cables, ducked under the big iron jig of the man who drilled the holes for the bomb racks, and tried not to step on any one of the succession of riveters who lay underneath the cat-walk and plugged up the holes that someone else had drilled.

These difficulties were nothing compared to being in a

ship when the bomb bay doors were being installed. The bomb bay doors, which were big shiny corrugated things, were put in by two men who always made us laugh when we saw them together. One was a big, dark, unsmiling fellow who looked out through his eyebrows and spoke with the most booming, pleasant voice we had ever heard. The other was a little, blond, smiling boy who came just to the big fellow's shoulder. After they fitted the big doors into place, they always had to test them by letting them fall shatteringly down against the cat-walk where C.M. was standing. *Crrrrr-ash!*

If Pappy's luck were really bad and his crew was "around the corner," there was an even greater horror than the bomb bay doors awaiting them. This horror was known as being "in the paint." First, four old women, who were the paper hangers, swooped down upon the ship, "like a flock of buzzards just peckin' a pore ole critter that ain't even daid yet," as Emeline put it. The paper hangers had strange tired voices like dust bowl mothers who had borne thirteen children, and they droned on all the time they were putting tape over the printed instructions and warnings and little arrows that were not to be painted. Then the painters themselves arrived, spraying the bomb bay with a dull gray paint that made even the air outside thick and foggy and hid all the familiar tubes and wires and brackets behind the same dull gray color.

It was things like these, said C.M. — back scrapers and elbow catchers and head bumpers, dural coming down and more and more people climbing in, bomb bay doors and paper hangers and painters; it was things like these, she said, one night at lunch (and I should have seen it coming!), that made her say the Black Hole of Calcutta was *nothing* compared to the Black Hole of Bomb Bay.

CHAPTER TWELVE

C.M. had scarcely seen Mr. Tompkinson since the first night when he had deposited her in the bomb bay under Pappy's care, and she was not quite sure now which one he was; but with Mr. MacGregor I had no such difficulty. He was the most omnipresent leadman in the building — except when I wanted to ask him something or get something from him. Then I had to wander forlornly down the line, peering up into the ships and asking the people working there, "Have you seen Mr. MacGregor?" They always said no, they hadn't and then asked curiously, "Who is Mr. MacGregor?" I explained that Mr. MacGregor was "Mac" and then they said, "Oh, — that slave driver!"

By the end of the first week I had decided that Mr. Mac-Gregor was a slave driver and that in time I, too, could grow to hate him. To begin with, he was a *neat* man. Now I am neat myself, even to my bottom bureau drawers; but I don't think a work bench should have to pass the white glove test. Mr. MacGregor did though. Mr. MacGregor was the sort of a man who could say he kept his motor as polished as the hood of his car. I told him I did too, which established a bond of sympathy between us, since I didn't explain that in my car it was the hood that was as polished as the motor.

Mr. MacGregor was always dusting the bench, straightening the things on it, and sweeping the floor around it. The first night I was there he asked me to sweep the floor. I did a beautiful job, sweeping out into the aisle on one side and over to the ship on the other. Later I learned that being asked to sweep was *the final insult*. Consolidated people terminated when they were asked to sweep the floor. They weren't hired to do janitor work, they said.

I, myself, felt like terminating one night when Mr. MacGregor told me to sweep up. I had been struggling all night with four different installations, one of them with the wrong wrench, so that I was nearly in tears at ten minutes to one.

"Are you through?" asked Mr. MacGregor, who in addition to his other faults had a disconcerting habit of optimism.

"All except the pulleys, and I can do those before the whistle," I said, rather optimistic myself.

"Only ten minutes," Mr. MacGregor reminded me cheerfully. "You'll *never* make it."

Remarks like that arouse my latent competitive spirit, and I always accept them as dares. This time I ran from ship to ship, right under the signs saying *"Positively No Running,"* while people gaped at me in amazement because such energy ten minutes before quitting time was practically unheard of. Every few minutes I asked someone what time it was and then said worriedly when he told me, "Oh dear!" or "That late?" or *"Only* four more minutes?" none of which was the normal response at that time of night. At last, breathless, I raced back to Station 20, thinking that Mr. MacGregor would at least pat me kindly on the head for the speed and dispatch with which I had performed my mission.

"The pulleys are in, Mr. MacGregor," I panted, restraining myself with effort from gasping, "Not wounded, sire, but dead," and slipping to the floor at his feet.

There was no pat on the head. No smile. No thanks.

"Sweep the floor," said Mr. MacGregor.

Another unpleasant thing about Mr. MacGregor was

that he ruled Station 20 on the principle that everybody should be able to build a bomber all by himself, or at least make all the Station 20 installations in one. During our first seven days on the Swing Shift while C.M. was doing one job in the bomb bay, I was making eight different installations, from safety belt holders to pipes. ("*Tubes*," corrected Mr. MacGregor; and when I asked him what the difference was he explained, "Tubes are smaller, lighter pipes." My calling tubes pipes, which I continued to do all summer, pained Mr. MacGregor, like my confusing the tail and the nose of the ship and saying bolt when I meant nut and nut when I meant bolt—only I usually called a bolt a screw, which was even worse in Mr. MacGregor's opinion.) The safety belt holders were considered a simple beginner's task at Station 20, but pipes (*tubes*) were No. 1 horrors.

My first experience with pipes was on my fourth night at work when Mr. MacGregor led me and another beginner down the line and "around the corner" to do "Parts Plant cleanup," in other words, to complete installations that should have been made at the Parts Plant. The pipes we were to install were asbestos-covered ones to be clipped in strange places at strange angles from the nose to the under flight deck. Our efforts to install and clip them must have been amusing; at least Mr. MacGregor laughed uproariously before he left us with optimistic instructions to finish three ships before one o'clock. We looked after him in such hopeless, helpless amazement—*Three ships?* —that a kind-hearted man stopped and asked, "Need some help?" We admitted that we did. He not only helped us—he *did* three ships for us so that we were able to return to Station 20 at one o'clock with our heads up. It was typical of Mr. MacGregor that he did not look the least bit pleased when we told him we had completed three ships. He didn't even look surprised.

The worst thing about Mr. MacGregor wasn't that he lay awake at night thinking up new horrors for my next job, but that he always presented me with the newest horror as if it were a special treat.

"I like to do this job myself," Mr. MacGregor would say, and then the job would turn out to be *pipes*. Or "I have a nice fellow for you to work with on this job," he would say, and the nice fellow would turn out to be some hopeless incompetent who was so far behind that he was working "around the corner." Then, having encumbered this already harassed man with my bungling services, Mr. Mac-Gregor would expect him to "catch up" with the line in one night.

On the fifth night Mr. MacGregor said cheerfully that he had a new job for me, a job he liked to do himself, working with a nice fellow too.

"Not *pipes*?" I said suspiciously.

Well, yes, Mr. MacGregor admitted, it was pipes, but *little* pipes. In my ignorance, I was relieved when he said they were little pipes. I did not know then that little pipes could be bent into many more strange and awkward shapes than big pipes. (The theory of bending the pipes before they were sent to us was that then they would fit around corners and over other installations. That was the *theory*. In practice, however, the pipes did not even faintly follow the line where they were supposed to be installed, mainly because by the time we were ready to put them up they had been stepped on by so many people that they were bent into entirely different and unexpected shapes. I agree with the girl who observed one night as I was struggling with a set of the little things, "Putting in pipes is awfully hard on your religion.")

After loading me down with little pipes, Mr. MacGregor took me into the bomb bay to show me a finished set, which consisted of four lines that ran to the gas gauge. (Four lines because there were four tanks to minimize the roll of the gasoline, Mr. MacGregor explained, when I said it was a lot of work just to show the pilot that he was out of gas.) The finished set looked very neat and gay, for the pipes were joined together by bright red and blue "unions," which were the color of Christmas tree decorations, and were marked with little red tapes to identify them as part of the gasoline system. They looked so cheery that I told Mr. MacGregor I thought I would like this job—better than the other pipes anyway. That was before I had seen "K-9" or Danny, who was the "nice fellow" I was to work with.

Danny was 18, with a protruding Adam's apple, slightly buck teeth, a sandy mop of hair, and a complexion that bore the retreating marks of adolescent acne. He had been installing the gas gauge pipes for three weeks, but he still looked vaguely at the four lines and said, "Let's see now," so bewilderedly that even when he finally announced happily, "That's it!" I was doubtful. He made frequent trips to the store room for various tools and pieces of equipment which he had forgotten; and quite often he looked at the set of pipes he had just installed and said at a quarter to one, with despair in his voice, "It's all wrong!"

Then in the end there was always "K-9." That was the number under which this particular section of the gas gauge system was listed on Mr. MacGregor's chart above the bench, just as all installations were listed by numbers; but K-9 was the only Station 20 installation so well known that its number had become a name. K-9, I found out later, had a reputation.

"Come on," said Danny the first night, as I was beginning to wonder if I hadn't been a little hasty in telling Mr. MacGregor I thought I was going to like the job. "I'll show you how to put in K-9."

He picked up a set of pipes and climbed up from the bomb bay to the flight deck, where there was a Brobding-nagian chair-like ladder that had been let down by the overhead crane through the opening for the top gun turret. I followed, climbing up the ladder and out on top of the fuselage of the ship. When I stood up, I was on the hump between the wings. It was a wonderfully free feeling after the crowded bomb bay, and I surveyed with pleasure the pattern of wing and fuselage which stretched in either direction down the line.

"I'm going to *like* working up here," I said confidently to Danny. As I spoke, the ladder on which we had climbed up was lifted from our ship by the overhead crane and swung easily down the line to the next one. Fasci-nated, I watched it moving away—and I wondered if I was going to like working on top of the ship.

"How," I said to Danny, but I tried not to sound wor-ried, only curious, "*How* are we going to get down?"

Danny did not appear to be worried.

"Oh, we can jump from this tail to that next wing and go down the ladder there," he said. "That's fun."

I looked down the length of the fuselage to the tail. The way the ships were arranged on the bias down the line, it was within jumping distance of the wing of the next ship. I wouldn't *exactly* call it easy jumping distance, and, besides, it was more than fifty feet down the fuselage to the tail and twenty feet to the floor on either side. It didn't look like too much fun to me.

I resolutely brought my eyes back and focused them on the hump where Danny and I were standing. At our feet were two small openings about a foot wide and three feet long. The doors to these openings were odd, I thought, because they curved in so that they would almost fill the space below which they were supposed to cover.

"What goes in there?" I asked Danny, trying to evince

an attitude of nonchalant interest and to forget how far it was to the floor.

"The life rafts," said Danny.

"Oh," I said, "isn't that an awfully inconvenient place to keep something you might want in a hurry?"

"You don't have to climb up on top of the ship and unpack them," Danny explained condescendingly. "See? They are stored in the hollows of those doors with wooden covers over them. When the ship starts down, you just pull a cord inside and bang! the doors spring open and throw off the covers. And there are the life rafts waiting for you. All inflated and everything."

I looked at the tiny doors respectfully.

"Now let's get to work," said Danny energetically.

"Yes, let's," I agreed, and I looked around for a suitable place to install K-9.

"You get in first," said Danny, picking up the pipes and standing aside for me.

"Get in where?" I asked.

"In there," said Danny. He pointed to the tiny door to the left of the hump.

"In *there*?" I gasped.

"Yes," said Danny, as calmly as if he hadn't asked me to perform the equivalent of climbing into my tool box. "That's where K-9 goes."

Obviously he was not joking. I looked at him sharply to be sure. Then I tentatively put one foot down through the door. I judged roughly that there might be room for my other foot. I put it down too.

"Now sit down," coached Danny helpfully. I sat down, using a special half twist to get my hips in. There was one terrifying moment when I thought I was going to be stuck forever in the top of that particular B-24. Out of breath, I finally wriggled myself loose and down into the compartment, tucking my head neatly under the edge of the opening. I breathed again, a deep breath, and looked around.

I was lying on the curving surface of the wings within the ship, and the surface felt as if it were composed mainly of huge rivets the size of nickels and dimes. My head was resting on the end of a metal cradle, which was comfortably padded in the center but knife-sharp on the end

"In *there?*" I gasped.

where it hit the back of my neck. My feet were twisted around the sharp end of a corresponding cradle. Above me, not six inches from the end of my nose, which is a pug one, was the top of the compartment. Along the top stretched neat complex rows of tubes and wires; and, imprisoned as I was, not sure whether I could ever wriggle out again to the freedom of the fuselage, these tubes and wires were my only comfort and hope. Men and women had climbed in and climbed out before. I was not alone. Danny slipped in beside me through the other opening with the dexterity of three weeks' experience, and pulled the pipes in after him. There were two sets of pipes ; and after putting them into position, he told me to take care of the set on my side. "Taking care of them" consisted of joining the pipes together with unions and clipping them to the beltframes they passed over. That was all — but I found out that there was a lot of difference between doing a job when I was standing up and it was at a comfortable distance and doing the same job when I was lying flat on my back and it was either at my nose's end or down around my knees.

I don't remember much about actually installing K-9 except that Danny kept telling me I would have a stiff neck the next day if I didn't quit sticking my head up through the small opening for air ; but I kept putting it out for a reassuring glimpse of the world and bringing it back to rest on Danny's shoulder when I had to drill a hole or manipulate a bolt through clip, washer and beltframe into the waiting nut.

This way it took the two of us thirty minutes to install the two small lines of tubes for K-9 with just one union and a couple of clips apiece ; but I thought as I struggled out that thirty days on the life raft itself couldn't be much worse than thirty minutes in the compartment where it was stored. I was battered and bruised and I bore on my back the print of a hundred rivets, nickel and dime-sized ones. I said to myself that the fairy tale princess who was bruised by one pea under twenty mattresses would have had an unpleasant time in the life raft compartment ; and when, the next day, Babe (of the bomb bay) told me that *she* liked to work in "the life raft," as she called it, because she could sleep there safe from the eyes of the Red Buttons,

I looked her over curiously, since it was my personal opinion that anybody who could sleep on those rivets would have to have the hide of a rhinoceros.

For myself, I thought putting in pipes, especially in "the life raft," was certainly hard on my religion. The language my tongue had wrapped itself around I shuddered to recall. There might be no atheists on rubber rafts, but it was a cinch there were no Christians in the compartments where they stored them.

CHAPTER THIRTEEN

EVERYBODY on the line seemed to know that C.M. and I were school-teachers.

In the first place, C.M. told them. She had a horror that they would know by looking at her that she was a school-teacher. So that they would not have a chance to guess (and since she didn't want them to think that we were ordinary aircraft workers anyway), she always told them our occupation the first thing — and then wondered unhappily how they knew.

In the second place, our former students told them. Our former students on the production line addressed us, to the amazement of the other workers, as Miss Bowman and Mrs. Allen; and they were frankly surprised to find us working on the Swing Shift, or to find us working at all, in fact.

"Have you given up teaching?" they asked.

"No," we explained, "we're here just for the summer."

"You ought to stay," they said seriously. "You'd make more money doing this than you do teaching." Sometimes they added, "Well — you teachers are finding out what it's like to work, aren't you?"

This last remark always sent me into a speechless fury or gales of laughter, thinking of five sets of themes a week, so that neither way could I answer; but C.M. always drew herself up to her full height of five feet two inches and pointed out that we considered working on the Swing Shift in an aircraft plant a *vacation*.

In the third place, our fellow workers found out for themselves that we were school-teachers by means of an extensive cross-examination to which we and all other newcomers were subjected. With me this cross-examination usually began when I was involved in an amateurish attempt at drilling a hole.

"Didn't you have to go to School?" some girl would ask wonderingly, School (with a capital) being the center for pre-factory training. (At first I did not understand this distinction and always answered yes, of course, I had gone to school.)

"No," I would admit, since it was probably painfully obvious that I had had no previous acquaintance with a drill motor.

"Don't they make you go to School any more?" she would ask persistently.

"Not if you're just a temporary worker," I would say, realizing that sooner or later this relentless cross-examination was going to pry my secret out of me.

"*Oh*—you go to school!" my examiner would say wisely, no longer capitalizing "school."

At this point I always tried to let the cross-examination stop right there by implying, without actually lying, that I did go to school. (Ye gods! Didn't I? Five days a week, forty weeks out of the fifty-two.) But then she would always ask what school and I never had the nerve, even after a haggard 18-year-old told me that she thought I was her age, to say that I *went* to San Diego High School. I always rather forlornly gave in and up.

"I teach school," I would say. "I teach high school. I teach high school English." Then I would pause dramatically for the silence that I knew would follow. There was always a silence when people found out I was a teacher, especially a high school-teacher—a high school English teacher. I think for a moment that they became young again and I became Miss Jones or whoever it was that used to rule their young lives.

By one of these three methods everybody on the line had found out that we were teachers. People from other stations asked us if we liked aircraft work better than teaching, mothers came to us for advice about their children who didn't like school, boys told us how they had left college after their first or second year to go into war work. *Everybody* recounted to us interminable tales of his own school days and the teachers he had liked and the teachers he hadn't liked, and *everybody* expounded to us his own theories on education. Mr. MacGregor told us proudly that his wife had been a home economics teacher and that she could make the *best* raisin pie — *with meringue on top.* Mr. Billings told us how he had taught in a one-room Indiana school with ninety kids from the first to the eighth grades.

"They ran me ragged," confessed Mr. Billings, "but I kept a bottle of 'bracer' in my desk for recesses."

Everybody knew we were school-teachers — everybody except Dusty. Dusty worked in the tunnel too, and he used to tell me his opinion of school-teachers, especially the ones that MacGregor assigned to help him install the tubing for the de-icer system. Dusty had been at Consolidated for a month and intended to quit in another month, but already he was hopelessly "around the corner" and Mr. MacGregor, without actually using somebody good on the job, kept trying to get Dusty back up to Station 20 by giving him all the new people as helpers. His first helper was a history teacher from a country school.

"Probably the reform school," growled Dusty to me as I was installing the safety belt holders and she was talking loudly about the advantages teaching had over aircraft work. She *loved* her children and her children *loved* her, she announced to Dusty and everyone else in the ship, including me. She and her children had *just lots of fun* together. She went on about the joys of teaching all the time Dusty was trying to explain her job to her. The job was installing tubing for the de-icer system, which kept ice from forming on the wings and tail of the ship. The tubing ran along the top of the tunnel from the tail through the life raft compartment. I thought it looked like a hard job — and so did she.

"Do I have to do *that* ?" she said. "Isn't that awfully dangerous ?" she asked, as Dusty straddled the open hatch and drilled a hole directly over his head ; "Isn't that awfully difficult ?" she inquired as he squeezed into the life raft compartment from the command deck ; and "Isn't that awfully dirty ?" she demanded as he smeared vaseline on the wired fittings. She seemed to be insulted that Mr. MacGregor had given her a job that was so dangerous, so difficult and so dirty.

Of course, it would be unprofessional for me to say anything against her ; but I was glad when she dropped a wrench and chipped her two front teeth that they weren't anybody else's front teeth. The night she dropped the wrench was her last night on the de-icer system. She asked Mr. MacGregor for another job, and after that I noticed that she held a bucking bar for a riveter. She terminated a week later.

After her came the Old Bitty, as Mr. MacGregor and Dusty called her behind her back. The Old Bitty was really a sweet character, a middle-aged teacher and the mother of a boy who was a member of a Liberator crew overseas ; but there was no place on the production line for a sweet character, unless she had sweet muscles too. The Old Bitty looked helpless, and she was helpless.

"Aw, give it to me, I'll do it," Dusty would finally say in disgust after she had arranged her paraphernalia and awkwardly mounted a stool to tighten the bulkhead fittings. She, too, disappeared after a week.

"School-teachers!" growled Dusty. "Don't I get nobody to help me but school-teachers? I'm going to ask MacGregor to let me have you for a helper, Darling," he confided to me. "I'm sick of school-teachers!"

A few nights later Mr. MacGregor announced with the air of one bestowing a great favor that he had a new job for me, a job he liked himself, he said, with a nice fellow, too.

"Pipes?" I said.

"Yes, tubes," he said. "The de-icer tubes with Dusty."

I did not know then that installing the de-icer was the kind of a job that made the other girls in Station 20 satisfied with whatever jobs they had. Later they told me that they'd even rather put in "the black stuff" than the de-icer. "The black stuff" was the synthetic rubber which was fitted around the gas tanks to absorb any gasoline that might leak out when the self-sealing tanks were hit in combat. It had a fragrance similar to that of rotten eggs. The girls in Station 20 detested the job, which was done by Pauline from Montana this summer, because the boys held their noses when they went by and said, "Whew! What kind of perfume are you wearing tonight?" I always thought that probably Mr. MacGregor was under the impression he had put me on "the black stuff" at some time, because otherwise I don't understand how he could miss such a satanic opportunity.

Nor did I know then that the girls in Station 20 would rather work by themselves than work with Dusty. Later they told me what I had by then discovered for myself: he was "fresh," he was slow, and he was lazy. He worked on the theory that Consolidated paid him by the hour, not by the ship. No matter how far down the line he was working, he was always in the ship at Station 20 when the whistle blew, his hands washed, his tools put away, and his box locked. The nearest I came to being killed this summer was one night when I was kneeling in front of Dusty at the entrance to the tunnel as the one o'clock whistle blew.

He'd served in the navy for 23 years, but he said somebody else could be the young hero of *this* war. Thinking that perhaps he had been the young hero of the last one, I asked him once if he had seen action then, but he admitted that he had not.

"By damn," said Dusty when I reported to him, "I'm sure glad MacGregor quit sending me school-teachers." The way he sneered "school" out, there might have been six "O's" in it.

I tried to be as un-school-teacherish as possible. I listened open eyed to his rather confusing explanation of how to install the de-icer system and I agreed wholeheartedly with his opinion of Mr. MacGregor, which was that the man was a slave driver.

"Darling," said Dusty, "you're better than any old school-teacher. We're going to get along, Darling!"

We did get along too — for three days — in spite of the fact that Dusty worked on the theory that the more he did the more that slave driver MacGregor would expect of him. Dusty did have a streak of rough chivalry in him. He always did the most difficult jobs. He put in the clip that had to go behind the oxygen bottles. He drilled the hole that had to be done with a fiendish "right angle" drill. *And* he put in the tube that went through the life raft compartment. He was always very nice about "the life raft," which I had never entered since my experience with K-9 and Danny. Although he said that being in the life raft with *him* was a thrill, he told me that if I didn't want to, I'd never have to climb up in that hole as long as old Dusty could climb up there for me.

During my first few nights on the de-icer, Dusty and I were hopelessly "around the corner" with the hot breath of Mr. MacGregor on our necks. Even when we finally got to the first ship on our side of the line before lunch one night, Mr. MacGregor pointed out that when the line moved at lunch-time we would be back on the other side. This did not worry Dusty a bit.

"That's why they pay MacGregor 10 cents extra an hour—to worry," said Dusty. "You and me, Darling, don't have nothing to worry about."

Dusty said he liked the other side of the line better anyway. There weren't so many people in our way. I, however, felt that being "around the corner" was a great shame ; and I worked out my usual complicated systems to speed us up. Every time I was near the storeroom I carried back a set of pipes for the next ship, even though we hadn't finished the one we were in. When Mr. MacGregor saw me with the pipes, of course he thought we were starting another ship and he was very pleased until I explained to him about my system. Even then, although disappointed, he was impressed by the system. The system didn't impress Dusty.

"Take it easy, Darling," he said as I struggled with the big wrenches I had to use to tighten the bulkhead fittings. "We've done enough for tonight." It did not worry Dusty that enough might be "too little" and tomorrow might be "too late."

"Slow down, Darling," he said as I tried to finish clipping the first pipe before the one o'clock whistle blew, "it'll wait."

Finally I decided that, slow and bungling though I was, we would get more ships done if we each had a definite part of the job to be responsible for. That way I could work as fast as I could and Dusty as slow as he wanted. I was anxious to get "around the corner" and back up to our station so that Mr. MacGregor couldn't point out to me that Sparky could install as many de-icer systems by himself as Dusty and I together. Besides, I was tired of being called "Darling."

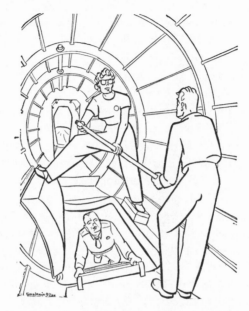

"Look, Dusty," I said, "Wouldn't you like . . ."

"Look, Dusty," I said, slipping school-teacher-like into suggesting a desired change by a question instead of a command, "wouldn't you like to do the nose half while I do the tail half? Wouldn't that be better?"

"Why, Darling," said Dusty, "you sound just like a school-teacher."

He looked at me suspiciously.

"You're not — are you?" he said hopefully.

"Yes, Dusty," I said gently. "I am."

"Oh, my god!" said Dusty. "*Another School-teacher!*"

And after that he never called me Darling.

CHAPTER FOURTEEN

M R. *MACGREGOR* was always very formal with a new girl; so when he climbed up into the tunnel one night with a girl obviously new, since she was still carrying her purse with her, he introduced me as "Miss Bowman" and her as "Miss Martin." (Usually he addressed me domineeringly as "Bowman," although I made a habit of calling him "Mister MacGregor," which title I personally considered a mild insult and he a strange mark of respect.)

"Miss Bowman will teach you how to install the safety belt holders, Miss Martin," Mr. MacGregor explained to the new girl.

"Miss Bowman will teach you —" I actually jumped. All of a sudden I was a teacher, not an aircraft worker. I was ready to give directions, ask questions, test knowledge acquired. I noticed the change in the way I stood, the way I answered Mr. MacGregor, and the way I appraised "Miss Martin." I think I felt the way Mr. Hyde must have felt when he suddenly turned back into Dr. Jekyll.

Miss Martin, whose first name was Lindy, looked like a Texas version of Loretta Young, lots of hair and lots of lipstick. She told me that she had gone to School for five weeks; in fact, she had already received the automatic nickel raise given at the end of the first month. She was actually making more money than I was, although I had been working on the line for three weeks. She also told me (this in a whisper) that she had worked six months at the Consolidated plant in Fort Worth before she came to San Diego, but "they" didn't know it.

"Gee, there are a lot of good looking men . . ."

I showed Lindy how the safety belt holders were assembled and installed. Sometimes her eyes wandered to other things and once she said as I was explaining how to space the bolts, "Gee, there are a lot of good looking men around here!" Showing the job to Lindy, I felt very experienced. I had sometimes amused myself by planning how I would teach the job to someone else with all the little tricks I had learned that made it easy. Later, at one o'clock, when I had bestowed a word of praise, for she had really done a good job her first night, Lindy looked at me admiringly and said, "Gee, you ought to be a school-teacher! You explain things so well."

"I *am* a school-teacher," I said, just to see her face.

Lindy and I became well acquainted this summer, for

she usually worked in the same ships I did. She'd quit high school when she was 15 to get married, and now at 18 she was divorced. She told me it hadn't "worked" because he was much older than she was. I asked how much older, picturing something like June and December. Well, Lindy said, he was *nineteen* — then, of course, there was the baby, not her baby, but the baby from his first marriage when he was seventeen.

"I've been through a lot," she said seriously.

I agreed that she had.

I liked Lindy in spite of her "flaming youth" story, for she was shrewd and humorous. She planned to re-marry her "Ex" when he came back from war ; she said she hoped they'd both have more sense then. He had sent her the old wedding and engagement rings, and she was wearing the diamond and "saving the other," she told me shyly.

Lindy lived in a trailer with her sister and brother-in-law, both of whom worked at Consolidated ; and she was very proud that during the last five weeks she had sent one hundred dollars back to her folks in Texas.

"My dad wrote that he knew I could spend it by the hundred but he didn't know I could save it the same way," she told me.

I suggested to Lindy that she should go back to high school and get her high school diploma. She lacked only a year's credits and she could get two credits for her work at Consolidated under the city schools' war-time "work experience" program.

Lindy looked interested.

"I'd like to have my high school diploma," she said, the way a girl says she'd like to have a mink coat.

The next night two girls asked me if it were true that they could get high school credit for working at Consolidated, and two others asked C.M. the same thing. In the next few days we were amazed to discover the number of girls on the line, many of them the most serious, hard working ones, who had not been graduated from high school. They all said like Lindy, a little wistfully, "I'd like to have my high school diploma."

Emeline, the girl who worked with C.M. in the bomb bay, had not finished school because there had not been enough children for a high school in the thinly populated section of New Mexico where she lived. She told us how she and her father had built a log cabin all by themselves and how she alone had fenced the homestead. The fence especially impressed C.M. and me because we were at that time unsuccessfully involved in hammering together wooden crosses for my mother's victory garden tomatoes. Emeline also told us how she used to "hire out" as a farm-hand with her father at the same wages he received and how one farmer came sixty miles to hire her because he thought she was worth any two men. Emeline's efficient, conscientious craftsmanship developed in C.M. a terrific feeling of inferiority, which was not offset even by Emeline's English, the world's worst and slowest. "Unconnect," for example, was one of Emeline's words; but by the end of the first week C.M. herself was saying "unconnect," at which Pappy would say mildly, "Unconnect what, Daughter?" When Emeline told me that she'd like to take English in high school, I said we could have a class of the Consolidated workers who had told me the same thing. Consolidated English 1A, we could call it.

"But not English like it's spoke here," Emeline cautioned.

Mary, a tiny girl who was one of the best workers on the line, had had to leave school in the ninth grade when her father died, leaving her mother with half a dozen younger boys and girls to support. Mary had gone to work in a preserve factory "to help out" although she was so young that the owner had to hide her when the state inspector came around. When the war started she and her younger sister had left Tennessee and come to California to get war jobs.

"I liked school," Mary said. "I didn't want to quit."

Nancy, who looked ridiculously young, healthy farm kid that she was, had left school to get married. Her husband (he looked *more* like her father) worked across the line in Department 194—although "they" didn't know that either.

I was not surprised that Nancy, young as she looked, was married. The Swing Shift was very domestic. It had to be. People who worked on the Swing Shift had to marry other people who worked on the Swing Shift because they never saw anyone else; and girls who were married to men on the Swing Shift had to work at the same time to see them at all. But I was surprised to learn that Nancy had two children.

"I'd like to get a high school diploma," she said, the way Lindy had said it, "but a mother of two children can't go back to high school."

Mattie, who had been a domestic servant before the war, had dropped out of school in the tenth grade because her step-father had felt that a girl of sixteen should be earning her own living. Now Mattie was 26.

"That's too old to go back to high school," she said.

She was a homely, quiet girl who worked in Department 140-Radio. When everybody on the line was kicking about the mere two cent raise he had received in the Wage Review and threatening to quit and saying disgustedly, "Consolidated can buy postage stamps with their damn two cents!" Mattie said quietly that she was making more money than she had ever made before or ever hoped to make again.

"I'm satisfied," she said.

Mattie had come "on nights" when her husband was shipped out to sea because, she said simply, the evenings were too long. She and the girl she lived with, whose husband was in Africa, gave themselves a "pep talk" every afternoon before they started off for work. Mattie said that they usually needed it.

Peg, from New Mexico, had quit school last year for the most common reason. She had come to California with her father and mother "to get a war job." C. M. and I thought that Peg was the most likely to finish her schooling. She was young and unmarried and only a year out of high school.

We tried to encourage all the girls to go back to get their diplomas, for we thought if they went in a group they would be more likely to stick it out. We told them how they could go to the continuation school and take only as many units as they thought they could handle, working as fast or as slow as they wished and receiving their credits whenever they completed the prescribed course of study; and we told them how many of our own students worked part-time at Consolidated during the school year. (I had so many riveters in my first period English class that I sometimes thought riveting must be the modern Fourth R of the famous Three.)

We don't know whether any of them really went back to school in September and if they did, how long they will stay. It would probably take more courage and determination and desire for learning than most of us have to go to school all day and work all night. But when high school girls come to us now and say, "I'm going to quit school," we tell them about the girls on the production line who did quit.

CHAPTER FIFTEEN

AT a quarter to one the news went down the line one night, from ship to ship and woman to woman, *"Everybody is out in front of the rest room."* "Everybody" was the Red Buttons of our department, standing guilelessly in conference at Station 18 just across the aisle from the women's room. As soon as they heard the news, the women stopped coming down to wash up, although there was usually a steady parade of them at a quarter to one. The last woman into the rest room announced in a stage whisper, "Hey, girls, the foremens are out in front!" There was a sudden series of flushing and zipping sounds in the twelve little cubicles, the walls of which bore various remarks about people who loafed on the toilets and people who were going to tell the foremen about them. The girls who had been relaxing in the little cubicles with their legs crossed came quickly out, and the girls who had been taking down their hair and starting over on the complicated arrangements of rolls and ribbons speedily put it up again. One by one they filed out by the fountain while Mr. Ely, Mr. Billings, Mr. Brown, Mr. Carter, and, this night, Mr. Plunkett himself, their red buttons very conspicuous, carelessly inspected each one as she emerged and tried to look as if they were discussing important Red Button business like increased production.

I watched the little drama from the window of my ship, which was at Station 18, and inspected Mr. Plunkett carefully so that I could describe him to C.M. Mr. Plunkett was *the* Red Button in Building Four, the assistant general superintendent in charge of B-24 production, and we had never seen him before. We had seen his office, the only closed office in the building, with his name in smaller letters under the name of the general superintendent "on days;" but we had never seen Mr. Plunkett himself. Sometimes somebody would say, "There goes Plunkett,"

There was usually a steady parade . . .

and we would turn to look; but he was always gone. During our first month at work we thought of him as an evil spirit brooding over the production line. This idea was fostered by information relayed to us by Emeline from her husband, who ran the overhead crane. He'd seen Mr. Plunkett, Emeline told us, he'd actually seen him lying on the balcony which ran above the line and peering down through the ships from tail to nose. After we heard that, we always felt as if Mr. Plunkett's omniscient eye were upon us ; and when the loud-speaker blared out, "Cuthbert J. Plunkett! Cuthbert J. Plunkett! Call ny-un, five, two-uh," we always expected a sudden darkening over the line and a rustle of wings as Mr. Plunkett passed by.

When I actually saw Mr. Plunkett in front of the women's room that night, I said, "Oh yes," the way I always say it when I connect a name with a face. He was the man in the brown suit, the short tanned man with the black hair greying at the temples, whom we had seen many times in groups of Red Buttons.

C.M. and I always referred to the Red Buttons and addressed them as "Mister," but all the other workers refused on principle to "Mister" anybody, "especially a Damn Red Button." (The way they said it, "Damn Red Button" was almost one word like "Damn Yankee.") Instead they always referred to the foremen simply by their last names, as Plunkett, Ely, Billings, Brown and Carter.

"I wonder what the foremen's first names are," said C.M. later as I was enlivening our vigil at the bus stop by describing the scene in front of the rest room. The last remnant of an English teacher left in me started to correct her for saying "foremens" like everybody else on the line ; then I remembered that she was using it possessively so it was all right.

"Well, it's Cuthbert J. Plunkett," I said and then I stopped. I couldn't remember having heard first names for Ely, Billings or the others. Neither could C.M. When we thought about it, there were many people we didn't have first names for and many we didn't have last names for, and there were some people we didn't have *either* first names *or* last names for, just nicknames. It was then that we evolved our *theory* of production line nomenclature: that the people on the line had just *one* name, first, last, or nickname, as far as the people who worked with them were concerned.

"The exception that proves the rule," said C.M. neatly, "is Mr. Plunkett. Everybody knows both his names because he's *important*."

We decided to test our theory the next night by asking the people we worked with if they knew the Red Buttons' first names; but first we decided to make it a guessing game for ourselves. Small things like that furnished amusement on the way home.

"Mr. Ely's name," said C.M., "should be Eli. Eli Ely. Of course, it's too good to be true," she admitted, and regretfully discarded Eli in favor of Lester.

I suggested Robert or Joseph for Mr. Billings — something that could sound pompous but wasn't really. For Mr. Billings' assistants, Mr. Carter and Mr. Brown, we selected Al and Hector. Mr. Carter was the only Red Button in our department who always wore a suit and a tie — always except *one* night, which wasn't even particularly hot, when he walked up and down the line in his shirt sleeves with his tie awry. Since this was the same night that Mr. Billings forgot his red button and appeared wearing an orange one with a big "T" for "temporary" on it, C.M. and I decided that there was obviously a *crisis* in the affairs of Department 192 and we were relieved the next night when Mr. Carter appeared with his coat and Mr. Billings with his red button. Mr. Brown, who had been nicknamed "The Bull o' the Woods" by the people under him, was the youngest Red Button in our department, a lad with a certain resemblance to a Great Dane recently out of puppyhood. Mr. Brown, young though he was, was living on more or less borrowed time. He was the assistant foreman I had narrowly missed with my motor my second night at work; and it was probably for this reason that he always side-stepped three or four feet whenever I passed. I mentioned this matter to Mr. Billings once when Mr. Brown went by me, circling wide.

"He probably thinks you dropped your motor on purpose," said Mr. Billings, who had no illusions about the affection the green buttons had for the red.

"Oh, but I didn't! I didn't even know he was a Red Button then!" I said brightly; and as my ears heard what my mouth said, I could feel my face turning as red as the red button which was blazing on the pocket of Mr. Billings' blue shirt.

It was making remarks like that and dropping motors on them that would make me a *great favorite* with the Red Buttons, C.M. said disgustedly when I told her about the conversation. She herself considered Mr. Brown the most eligible man on the line, mainly because he looked like her brother. When he came into the bomb bay she conversed with him quite sociably as if she were wearing skirts instead of slacks. Mr. Brown, however, was very businesslike. He said he was trying to get acquainted with some of the personnel in the electrical department. C.M. said (to me later) that it was funny to be thought of as a personnel instead of a person.

We learned Mr. Carter's and Mr. Brown's first names quite easily. We had asked only half a dozen people when Mary contributed the information that Mr. Carter's name was Al. C.M. and I shrieked happily and congratulated ourselves on our choice. C.M. said that Mr. Carter's mother must have been a remarkable woman to name him Al even before he began to wear shirts and ties that blended with his suits. Then Blondie (from Texas) told us that Mr. Brown's name was Cor-ul.

"Coral?" we asked.

"No, Cor-ul," she said.

Later we saw it in print and it was Carl.

Mr. Billings' and Mr. Ely's first names were much more difficult to learn.

"What's Mr. Billings' first name?" C.M. and I would say to each person who came into the ship where we were working.

"Gosh, I don't know," he would say, adding helpfully, "Everybody calls him Bill."

"Yes, but what's his first name?" we would persist.

"Gosh, I've *heard* it!"

"And what's Mr. Ely's first name?" we would ask.

"Gosh, I've never even heard *that*!"

For three weeks we asked each person who came into the ship and the people we had asked asked other people. "What's Billings' first name?" and "What's Ely's first name?" Always the answers were the same : "Gosh, I've *heard* it!" to the first one and "Gosh, I've never even heard *that*!" to the second.

During the course of our investigation into the first names of the Red Buttons, we found that the general attitude toward them was a mixture of contempt and fear. Contempt because the Red Buttons wore clean clothes and didn't do anything, and the ordinary worker on the line could not comprehend the idea of being paid to assume responsibility. Contempt, also, because the Red Buttons played "politics"—for neither could the ordinary worker comprehend the idea of appointing a man to a position because he had the ability to get other men to work. The fear of the Red Buttons was something which we did not understand. As another teacher who was working on the other side of the line said, "The foremen won't let them leave their jobs now and after the war they'll be out of their jobs anyway—so what's their worry?"

The fact that we asked the Red Buttons for information and instruction amazed our fellow workers and worried our leadmen. Every time Mr. MacGregor saw me talking to Mr. Billings he would come up afterwards and ask, "What's the matter? Did Billings catch you when you were having trouble?"

I achieved a minor notoriety one night by calling upon Mr. Billings to show me how to use a right angle drill, an instrument which I had never seen before. Mr. Billings climbed gingerly up to the command deck, gingerly being the way Red Buttons always climbed into the ships, since they were afraid they would get their suits dirty. As he climbed in, I could hear the two girls in the tail fluttering in horror, "Imagine! Asking a Red Button how to do something!" Well, I thought, a Red Button *ought* to know how to use a right angle drill.

Mr. Billings took the drill, which was an ugly long affair to make holes in out-of-the-way places like behind the oxygen bottles, and explained to me that I must *never* start my motor until I had a firm grip on the right angle. Otherwise it would spin madly, twisting itself out of shape and wreaking much havoc on me and everything around me. He took a firm grip on the drill and flipped on the motor. Nothing happened.

"I guess I forgot to connect it," I said apologetically, while the girls in the tail giggled. Mr. Billings looked patient. While I tried to untangle the cord and follow it through to the plug, he went on to explain that electric motors were very dangerous things, that a right angle drill was especially dangerous, and that I should never turn on my motor unless I had a *firm* grip on the drill. As he said this, he was absent-mindedly flicking the switch on and off. Just as I found the end of the cord neatly planted in the plug and turned to tell Mr. Billings that there must be something wrong with the motor, it suddenly decided to work.

Mr. Billings was quite right.

Nobody should ever turn on the motor unless he has a

firm grip on the right angle. Blushing, Mr. Billings returned my twisted and broken drill to me.

"You see," he said, the way a teacher turns an error to
her own advantage, "that's what happens if you don't have
a *firm* hold on the drill when you turn on the motor."

After Mr. Billings had disappeared down the hatch, the
girls in the tail gleefully congratulated me. They were
as pleased as they had been when I dropped my motor on
Mr. Brown.

"Them foremens," said one disgustedly.

"Damn Red Buttons," said the other.

It was their opinion that there were Too Damn Many
Damn Red Buttons.

"A lead man for every two men, and a foreman for every
four men," said one.

"Yeah," said the other, "we hear a lot about a manpower
shortage, but nobody puts the Red Buttons to work. Look
out there — *five*," she said disgustedly, "and here comes
Plunkett, that's *six*."

There were at least three dozen Red Buttons in our
building; and it usually seemed like more because they
were omnipresent, walking up and down the line all night.
When a Red Button looked up into the tunnel, everybody
stopped talking and worked diligently. ("Red means
Stop," observed Lindy one night, "but these Damn Red
Buttons mean Go.") There was a very efficient Red Button warning system so that rarely did one arrive un-
heralded. "Here come the foremens," somebody would
say, "foremens" being the southwestern plural of foreman.
The Red Buttons had a high visibility anyway because besides the red button there were the polished shoes, pressed
trousers, suit coat, and slick hair so that a person could tell
from any part that the whole was a Damn Red Button.

Every time a Red Button would look up into the ship,
we would remember to ask the others working with us,

"What's Billings' first name?" and "What's Ely's first name?" One night somebody told us that Mr. Billings' first name was Benny. Benny Howard or Harris, maybe Harrison. Something like that anyway.

"Undoubtedly it is Benjamin Harrison Billings," said C.M. positively. "Mrs. Billings would name all her children after presidents. Mr. B's brothers are undoubtedly named George Washington Billings and Abraham Lincoln Billings."

The only trouble with this idea was that when we computed with much difficulty how many years it was since Benjamin Harrison had been president of the United States, we decided that Mr. Billings couldn't possibly be that old and we couldn't imagine anyone, even Mrs. B., naming a child after Benjamin Harrison unless he was president at the time of its birth. Still, it was a good name for him — Benjamin Harrison Billings, and then Benny Billings.

Mr. Ely's name was still a mystery. We had found out that his first initial was "L." At least, we *thought* it was L. The signature on the tool purchase permit was a little hard to decipher. An "L" meant that his name *could* be Lester, as we had guessed.

"There is only one thing to do," I told C. M. after we had asked several hundred people if they knew Mr. Ely's first name. "We'll just have to ask Mr. Ely himself."

"Let's ask Mr. Billings first," she suggested. "What do you bet he doesn't know it either?"

After 11 o'clock "smokin" we approached Mr. Billings.

"Mr. Billings, we have a question to ask you," I said seriously. Mr. Billings looked serious too. "*What* is Mr. Ely's first name?"

Mr. Billings looked a little surprised, but he looked as if he knew the answer. I looked at C.M. She looked at me. Here it came!

"It's Eli," said Mr. Billings.

"Eli?" we gasped in unison. *"Eli Ely?"* It was too good to be true. Eli Ely. Our first guess.

Yes, Mr. Billings explained, Mr. Ely was a twin. He was Eli and his brother was Levi. Eli and Levi Ely.

We thanked Mr. Billings happily, explaining to him about the theory and the guessing game. He wanted to know what name we had selected for him, and we told him about Robert and Joseph.

"It's Benny Herbert," he said.

"Benjamin?" I asked hopefully.

"No," he said definitely. "Benny."

Our disappointment that Mr. Billings' name wasn't Benjamin Harrison Billings was lost in our delight with Mr. Ely's name. Eli Ely! With joy we spread the news through the ships we worked in that night. Eli Ely! By one o'clock everybody had heard the news and greeted us with, "How do you like what Mr. Ely's name turned out to be? Eli Ely!"

We were quite happy about it until I got another look at Mr. Ely's red button one night. The red buttons had the owners' names and positions on them. There it was: L. *Ely*, Assistant General Foreman, Department 192.

"Do you think," I asked C.M. forlornly, "that Mr. Billings was confused? That Mr. Ely is Levi and his twin is Eli?"

"Probably Mr. Billings was completely confused," said C.M. sourly. After all, it was quite a blow. "Probably there are no Ely twins. Probably Mr. Ely is both Levi *and* Eli."

Levi Eli Ely. That was even better. I said the whole thing just proved our theory. *Nobody* on the line had both a first name and a last name, except Mr. Plunkett. Even the foreman didn't know his own general foreman's first name.

"I'm going to ask Mr. Ely," I said, "although I doubt if he will know himself."

I did ask him too.

"What's your first name, Mr. Ely?" I asked.

"Lee," he said.

Was it Lee for Eli or Levi? Was there an Eli Ely or a Levi Ely? Was there a twin? Did Mr. Billings make the whole thing up? Did Mr. Ely know his own name?

Sometimes now, when our fingernails have grown back and our callouses have worn off and we have started to react to bells instead of whistles, we still wonder.

CHAPTER SIXTEEN

THE quitting whistle blew at one o'clock, and at five minutes after 1 by the time clock almost every card had been taken from the "In" rack, punched, and put into the "Out" rack—every card except those of the men who were working overtime, and Bowman's and Allen's. This impressed the foremen, confused the timekeepers, amazed our fellow workers, and aroused the suspicions of the guards at the gate.

"I wish more people would stay around the way you girls do," said Mr. Billings, much impressed when we crossed the over-pass with him at 1:30 one night. Mr. Billings loved to stay around himself.

"Oh, no, you don't, Mr. Billings!" we said. "Besides, the timekeepers wouldn't stand for it."

We explained to him then how we, single-handed, were putting a small snag into the timekeeping system of Department 192. When we finally arrived at the time clock each night, our timekeeper was standing there looking forlornly at our two cards which she had stuck up invitingly in the rack for us. She smiled patiently when we handed them back to her and wrote N. O. T. beside 1:18 or whenever it was that we were checking out. That meant "Not Over Time." We felt very virtuous about punching out so late each night until some cheerful creature in the bomb bay told C. M. that a person who punched out after 1:10 was penalized just as much as if he were late to work. That was Big Business for you—mad if you came late, mad if you went late. But that night we got down to the time clock by 1:03 and breathlessly demanded of the head timekeeper if it were true. She said no, not exactly, but the timekeepers were authorized to take the cards from the rack at 1:10 and penalize the owners two-tenths of a day's pay for not punching out just as they would be penalized for not punching in. When we realized that our timekeeper had waited for us night after night past the legal last minute, we were conscience-stricken and C.M. promised for both of us that we would always punch out by 1:10 after that. We were very fond of our timekeeper, who was a real gentlewoman. After that we went through the complicated procedure of packing C.M.'s tool pocket into my already bulging tool chest, washing our hands and arms up to the sleeves of our T-shirts, and putting on our faces at Mr. MacGregor's bench (*much* to his disgust) in the record time, for us, of nine minutes and thirty seconds.

The fact that we punched out at 1:10 did not mean, however, that we went home at 1:10. Not us. There were too many things we wanted to see. Walking the distance from Building Four to Gate Two was like going home at closing time from the county fair. Our feet had the same too-much-stood-upon ache. In front of us was the crowd heading toward the brightly lighted gates where newsboys were shouting their wares. Along the way were huge piles of boxes that looked as if fascinating exhibits had been unpacked from them. The half-opened doors of the buildings, looming big and dark under the net of camouflage, gave hints of bright lights and exciting things within. We couldn't resist. Off we went on some small expedition to peek in at the Coronados or the Catalinas, to watch the arc-welders, or to explore the finished B-24's at the end of our own line.

Our enthusiasm for going every place we could go and

127

seeing everything we could see amazed our fellow workers —although I suspect the fact that we were willing to use our own time instead of company time was what really amazed them. We came early so that we could go for a ride in the overhead crane with Emeline's husband, and we stayed late so that we could walk down to the end of the production line. We were delighted when we had to make a trip to another building to buy tools, have an injury treated or order safety glasses. When our lead men sent us on some errand down the line, we accepted the commission with such alacrity that they looked after us dizzily.

But at last we had gone up and down the line so many times that the only thrill was at the door with the first ship on our right and the last ship on our left. There were just two things we were determined to see before we left: the Coronado production line and the Catalina line. Realizing these ambitions was not easy, for we were supposed to stay in our own department and our button announced in big numbers that our department was 192.

We finally saw the Coronados on their line when we went to order our safety glasses; luckily, the week before the safety crib had been moved to that building. As we entered, the place seemed so deserted that we wondered if everybody had gone home. The Liberator line was never that quiet except between shifts in the afternoon. Our first impression, after the quiet, was of lovely greyed colors, blues and greens and yellows. After the colors, we saw the ships, which stretched down one side of the building. They were so big that we actually hadn't seen them at first. The depth of the hull, the spread of the wings, even the size of the double-finned tail overwhelmed us. The Coronados were as big as we had expected the *big bombers* to be.

The man at the safety crib was very pleased that we were impressed by "his" Coronados, for next to his enthusiasm for safety glasses was his pride in those flying boats. First he showed us half a dozen photographs of smiling workers behind cracked but unshattered safety glasses which had been hit by flying drills and falling wrenches; then he offered to show us the Coronados.

"Are you sure it will be all right?" we asked timidly, half expecting to feel the strong grip of the F. B. I. on our shoulders.

"Oh, sure," he said. "Come on."

As we passed people who were working on various sub-assembly jobs, he explained that the line of ships we had seen down the side of the building was the equivalent of our production line and that the Coronado sub-assembly work which was being done in the building was done for the Liberator line at the Parts Plant. He told us proudly how many Coronados were turned out in a week and we said scornfully that we built that many Liberators in a day. We had to admit, however, that our ships weren't as big as his. The Coronados were enormous. When he showed us the keel being laid for one, it looked like the keel of a ship.

"I wouldn't have *any* trouble calling these ships ships," said C.M., who still slipped sometimes and said "planes." ("They are planes, aren't they?" she always said plaintively when I corrected her.)

"These *are* ships," said the man from the safety crib. "They fly and they float."

After we had visited the Coronados, we wanted more than ever to see the Catalina line. We even asked Mr. Billings if there wasn't *something* we could order in the Catalina building.

"No," he said, "but you see the Catalinas outside every day on your way to work."

"Oh, Mr. Billings," we said disgustedly, "that isn't the same thing at all!"

That night on our way to the gate, we stopped to look at the finished Coronados and Catalinas lined up outside Buildings Two and Three. C.M. admired the snooty dowager look of the big Coronados, but I liked the sleek fish-like lines of the Catalinas.

C.M. admired the snooty dowager look . . .

"A Catalina looks like an airplane carrying a boat," I said to C.M. as we stopped in front of one.

"Or a sea gull carrying a fish," she said.

"But it's a *sweet* ship to fly," said somebody behind us. It was a young fellow smoking beside the sign that said "No Smoking." He had on a red, white and blue button so we knew that he was a navy inspector. He looked at the Catalina proudly and shook his head. "It was obsolete when it was first built, but it's still the best ship the navy's got," he said.

"How do you get into it?" we asked practically, for it had no hatch like the B-24.

"Through those blisters on top," he said, pointing to two plexiglass coverings that did look like blisters. "That's the only way."

"May we look inside?" I asked hopefully, because he was still smoking his cigarette and seemed inclined to talk.

"Not in that one. The navy inspector has sealed it for delivery and no one can get in until the navy breaks the seal. But come inside," he said, carefully putting out his cigarette, "and I'll show you through one on the line.

"You will!" we shrieked. "But will it be all right? The F.B.I. won't mind?"

"Oh, sure, it'll be all right," he laughed easily and led us inside.

Our first feeling was that we had entered an aquatic museum, for the line of Catalinas was strung along in front of us, tail of one to the nose of the other, like a row of stuffed sharks. We followed the inspector up to a ship that had no blisters yet, climbed the ladder, and dropped down into the ship. Although it was much smaller than a B-24, it gave an impression of greater length because we could see all the way through, compartment after compartment, from tail to nose. What it really looked like was something that a cannonball had gone straight through.

"Just wait till we tell Mr. Billings that we went through a Catalina," crowed C.M. gleefully after we had thanked the inspector, who laughed at our excitement. "Looking at them outside — huh!"

When we finally arrived at the gate and showed our lunch boxes to the guard, he looked at us suspiciously as if he thought we were carrying off a bomber bit by bit in them.

"Were you working overtime?" he asked as we closed our lunch boxes.

"Are you joking or asking?" I said, not at all sure because that was what everybody said when we hung around after one o'clock to look at things.

"I'm *asking!*" he said, and from the look on his face I knew that he was.

"We *are* a little slow getting out," C.M. admitted shamefacedly.

The guard looked at the clock on the side of the building, which amazed us by showing five minutes to two, and said sarcastically that he thought fifty-five minutes was a little *too* slow.

"We were just looking around," I gulped.

"That's just what you're *not* supposed to do," said the guard sternly.

He looked at us so searchingly that we felt like apprehended agents of the Gestapo. He even said *something* about the F. B. I.

"Now, don't let it happen again," he ended weakly.

We said no, sir, we wouldn't, sir, and thank you, sir.

Afterwards we never could remember just what he had said about the F.B.I., but we were sure he had *mentioned* it ominously. The next day when Emeline's husband told us he would take us for another ride in the overhead crane after one o'clock, we said regretfully that we were sorry but we couldn't go. We had to get out of the plant *quick* at one o'clock. We warned him and all our other friends on the line that if an F.B.I. man came around to investigate us, they were to tell him how hard we worked and how many war bonds we bought.

"I knew you-all would have the F.B.I. on you-all if you-all didn't watch out," drawled Emeline. (Even though upset, I made a mental note that that was the only time I had ever heard anyone actually say "you-all" three times in one sentence.)

Riley, who had more or less adopted us for the summer,

escorting us to the gate whenever we went out reasonably near one o'clock, said deliberately that if the F.B.I. came around to *him,* he was going to tell them a thing or two about sabotage.

"But we're not saboteurs, Riley!" we wailed. We were not too sure of Riley because we had practically ruined *his* reputation by announcing in loud voices one night that Mr. Billings was simply *raving* because Riley had crossed the wires in the bomb bay and made the red lights green and the green lights red. Riley had explained seriously the next time we saw him that he had nothing to do with the red and green lights, and anyway the red lights were red and the green ones green because they were covered with red or green glass. That just made it worse, we had told him. That was just why Mr. Billings was hopping.

"Yes, sir," said Riley, savoring the last delectable spoonful of fresh apricot jello he had brought in his lunch, "I'd tell the F.B.I. a thing or two about sabotage. There's plenty of that around here — time wasted, material wasted, *and* work done wrong the first time so that it has to be done over.

"Yes, sir, I'd just *like* to have the F.B.I. ask me about sabotage," said Riley, who drew a fabulous pay-check each week for doing over what other people had done wrong.

CHAPTER SEVENTEEN

OUR own personal production index was the chart of Station 20 installations which was tacked up above Mr. MacGregor's bench. Along the top of it were the numbers of the ships on the line, and down the side were the numbers of the twenty-some installations made by Mr. MacGregor's crew. As soon as an installation was completed in a ship, a stamp was placed in the appropriate square, a red stamp for a day crew ship and a black stamp for a night crew ship. There were a great many squares to be stamped, for the chart was six or seven feet long; but the thing that impressed us was the surprisingly short time that elapsed between the day that a new chart went up and the day that it came down with all the squares stamped. It always gave us the satisfying feeling that we were really accomplishing something.

One afternoon, however, when I arrived at Station 20, I found Mr. MacGregor scowling at the chart, which looked like my crossword puzzles when I have filled in everything except the 14-letter scientific terms and the 12-letter national folk epics of the ancient Phoenicians.

"Is something wrong?" I inquired politely.

Mr. MacGregor snarled.

"Is something wrong?" he demanded. *"Is something wrong?* Just look at that chart." He pointed despairingly to the blank squares. "No tubes for K-9. No pulleys for F-8. No cables for K-12. I can't stamp off one of those damn installations because every one of them is *short !"*

"Oh," I said, suddenly reminded of something. "I forgot to tell you — the de-icer system is short, too. There aren't any more of those tubes that go behind the oxygen bottles. I noticed on my way over."

"Oh my god!" said Mr. MacGregor. *"Oh my god!* Last week it was short on one end. The week before it was short on the other end. Now it's short in the middle. *Oh my god!"*

Mr. MacGregor continued to say "Oh my god!" at regular intervals during the next few days, for that was the week that nearly every Station 20 installation was "short" one part. Every night Mr. MacGregor inspected the shelves in the storeroom, which looked as bare as Mother Hubbard's cupboard, and said unhappily that everybody at Station 20 would be "on the field" by the end of the week.

Whenever a part was "short," everybody continued to make his installations, doing as much as he could without the missing cable or tube or pulley. The ships continued around the line, out the door, and onto the field with a tag saying "Shortage — Parts to Be Installed Here" hung where the missing part was to go. When the part came in, he went out on the field or down to the door or around the corner, wherever the first ship with the part missing was, and worked his way back around the line to Station 20.

Toward the end of the week some of the "short" parts began to come in from the "feeder plants" up the coast. They were delivered direct to the bench with big green tags saying *"Rush"* and big white tags bearing the name of the feeder plants — Laguna Beach, Santa Monica, Pasadena, wherever it was. The "short" de-icer tube, however, did not come in; and Mr. MacGregor said gloomily that if that damn tube didn't come in by tomorrow Dusty and I would have to go out on the field to install it.

"Really!" I said, mentally clapping my hands. "Really out on the field?"

"*Really* out on the field!" Mr. MacGregor mocked me. "Really out on the field, where it's dark and cold and wet and everything is in your way."

"But it won't be cold and wet in August," I objected, in defense of the San Diego climate.

"That's *all right*," said Mr. MacGregor ominously. "It will be dark, and everything will be in your way."

I knew it was practically sabotage, but I couldn't help wishing that the "short" tube would not arrive the next night so that Dusty and I could go out on the field and work in a ship that was all finished — except for the de-icer tube. It didn't arrive the next night, and the first ship that Dusty and I had done without it was at the next to the last station on the line. The next time the line moved it would be out on the field!

"Bowman!" said Mr. MacGregor irritably, looking up from the daily letter which the leadman on days always left. "Take a wrench and tighten the fittings you left loose for that short tube. You'd better tape over the ends of the other tubes too so that the dirt won't get in them. That damn thing may never come in, and I've got to check something off this chart." (The de-icer system was listed on the chart as two separate installations, the nose half and the tail half; and if the last fitting for the nose half were tightened, that installation could be checked off as complete even though the tail half was still short one tube.)

"I guess Dusty and I will get to go out on the field," I observed happily.

Mr. MacGregor growled and looked fiercely at the blank spaces left on the chart above the bench.

Armed with a big roll of adhesive tape and three heavy

wrenches, I set off gaily, for a trip around the line was always interesting. On my way I stuck my head into the bomb bay where C.M. was working and announced impressively what Mr. MacGregor had said. The tube might *never* come in. C.M. was horrified too, because we both had a mental picture of the almost completed B-24's being left forever on the field because they were short one de-icer tube, or else being sent out with a gap in the de-icer system so that the harried little co-pilot would have to scramble out on the wings and chip the ice off with a small domestic ice-pick.

I also stopped at the First Aid Station for a few minutes. I explained to the nurse that I was going to tighten many fittings and that when I tightened fittings I usually cut my fingers or scraped my knuckles on the rivets of the seventh bulkhead. (There's many a Liberator in the air today with bits of my flesh clinging to its seventh bulkhead. Incidentally, I found out when I went back to school this fall that these murderous rivets had been put in at the Parts Plant by one of the students in my second period English class, and it took all my self-control to keep from flunking the boy.) I asked the nurse if she would tape all the fingers of my right hand, from the base to the tip, to protect them from the rivets. She looked at me, looked at the fingers of my right hand, and looked confused.

"Did you say that you cut your fingers?" she asked helplessly.

"No," I explained, "I just expect to cut them."

I repeated what I wanted her to do, and after a period of deliberation she decided to comply with my request. As she taped the five fingers of my right hand, she said with a worried frown that she didn't know quite how to report this in her record book.

"It isn't an injury," she said, "because you haven't injured yourself yet."

"Put it down as Preventive Medicine," I suggested, as I set out for the next to the last ship.

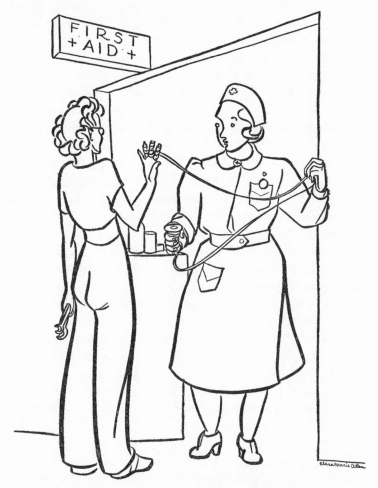

"Put it down as Preventive Medicine!"

Behind the noises of the production line I could hear a deep musical overtone like the opening notes of a great symphony played poorly on a poor French Horn. On my way to the next to the last station, I stopped in front of the ship from which the sound was coming. The rubber cover on the edge of the wing was expanding and contracting in alternate tubes as the three notes blared forth.

"What makes that noise?" I asked the man standing on the platform under the wing.

"That's the de-icer," he explained. "We're testing it."

"The de-icer!" I exclaimed. "Golly, I put in the pipes for the de-icer."

The man remained unimpressed by this news, but he took time to explain the mechanics of the de-icer to me. The tubes in the rubber cover on the edge of the wing and the tail were expanded and contracted by compressed air units in the motors, he told me. The rubber cover was called a "boot" and the tubes were called "lungs." I watched proudly while the "lungs" on the edge of the wing rose and fell to the three loud notes.

"It's an awful noise, isn't it?" asked a woman who had stopped to watch with me.

"Listen, that's music," I said indignantly. "That's the de-icer system I put in."

The woman looked impressed, even if the man hadn't, and said, "My! Is it really?"

As I continued on my way down to the next to the last ship, I hummed the theme of a "de-icer symphony" I had just decided to compose some day. Mmm. Mmmmm. Mmmmm. Just those three notes that the de-icer made.

When I climbed into the next to the last ship on the line, I felt a sudden surge of wanderlust. It was so obviously all ready to go places! Everything was dusted and in its place. Piled high in the tunnel were packages, boxes, bags and suitcases. I had to climb over them to get to the seventh bulkhead. I tightened the bulkhead fittings that had been left loose on either side of the space where the "short" tube was to go, and then I taped the ends of the tubes that were already up with a very intricate arrangement of adhesive tape so that not even the smallest particle of dust could get in. Thinking of Mr. MacGregor, I gave the fittings an extra twist with the wrench. Nothing, absolutely *nothing*, made Mr. MacGregor madder than to have an inspector refuse to pass something Station 20 had installed because it wasn't tight enough.

I asked an inspector who was making a final check with a little list in his hand how the inspectors tested fittings to see if they were tight.

"With our fingers," he said. "The Finger Test, we call it."

"Well," I said, gritting my teeth for a final turn with the wrench and practically swinging on the fitting, "it will take a finger of iron to find that this one's loose."

After all, Mr. MacGregor's last words had been : "Get them *tight*, Bowman !"

I climbed into ship after ship around the line, skipping the alternate groups that had been done by the day shift. I tightened the bulkhead fittings until they squeaked their protests. I taped the open ends in masterful fashion. I did every night shift ship on the line except the one where the man was testing the de-icer system. In that one he had rigged up a short hose across the gap left by the missing tube so that he could run the compressed air from the nose to the tail. Finally, at two minutes to eleven, I staggered up to Station 20 ; and while the people along the way looked sympathetically at my bandaged fingers, I tried to figure out how with all five fingers bandaged from base to tip I had still been able to cut one finger and scrape one knuckle. (Only I *could* do it, according to C.M.)

At Station 20 Mr. MacGregor was re-reading his letter from the day shift leadman and muttering, "If he can't take people off their regular jobs to fill shortages, how does he think I can ?" and "If he needs five more workers, how many more does he think I need ?"

"The fittings are all tightened and taped, Mr. Mac-Gregor," I announced, thinking to cheer him with this good news. "Every one of our ships on the line —— "

I stopped. On the bench in front of Mr. MacGregor was a pile of tubes (How well I knew them !) with a big green "*Rush*" tag on top.

"After smoke-time, you and Dusty can take off the tape and loosen the fittings," said Mr. MacGregor, "and put these in."

After smoke-time Dusty and I did put them in, starting out at the next to the last ship on the line. And Dusty said that he had never seen such *neat* tapings or such *tight* fittings. This last he said between clenched teeth as the perspiration streamed down his face.

We didn't get out on the field that time, but I made Mr. MacGregor *promise* — and I periodically reminded him of his promise — that he would send me out to work on the field before I left.

"I *promise*," said Mr. MacGregor, laughing fiendishly.

A week or two later another de-icer tube was "short" ; and before it finally came in, every ship on the line and a few on the field were without that tube.

"Here you go, Bowman," chortled Mr. MacGregor as he piled the tubes high in my arms. "Here you go out on the field. Remember you *asked* to go !"

"Yeah," said Dusty, who was loaded down with a flash-light, a tool chest, and a stool. "You *asked* to go."

As we went outside through the wire gate with "No Admittance" on it, Dusty pointed out to me that we would probably be "around the corner" all the next week because of the time we would lose installing the "short" tubes.

Out on the field there were a dozen or so Liberators lined

up along the fence. This was what was called Bomber Row. Dusty and I walked down the row to the last ship, Dusty grumbling all the way. The last ship was dark inside, but he climbed up into the tail and felt for the de-icer tube. It was in. I climbed up into the next ship and felt for the tube. It was in too. We continued back down the row like that until we came to a ship where it was missing. That was where we were to start and then work our way down Bomber Row, around the line, and back to Station 20 eventually.

While Dusty went back into the building to get some-thing he had forgotten, I flashed my light around the inside of the tunnel. It looked beautifully clean and neat after the confusion of the line. I was pleased to see that all the holders we had installed were holding things — safety belts in the safety belt holders, a compass in the compass brack-ets, a sens-antenna in the sens-antenna straps.

As long as Dusty was taking his time about getting the wrench, I decided to explore. I climbed around the belly turret and down under the command deck into the bomb bay, which with the bomb bay doors down was really a black hole. By my flashlight I could see that the back half had huge cargo bunks on either side of the cat-walk although the front half was empty. Above the cargo bunks were check lists for the various things that were to be packed in them. From the bomb bay I climbed up to the flight deck, where my flashlight startled me by lighting up the word *"Face"* in large white letters. Dusty ex-plained to me later that this indicated the hard side of the armor plate, which was turned away from the pilot so that the bullets would not hit it and fly back at him.

A man who looked like Gary Cooper (but not enough to be exciting) was sitting in the co-pilot's seat, testing the safety devices at the instrument panel, which glowed softly in the dark under the invisible ultra-violet light above him. I climbed up beside him and sat in the pilot's seat before an enormous number of buttons and switches that had little plastic ridges on each side of them to guide the pilot's fingers while his eyes were on something else.

"Golly," I said, studying the specific instructions and warnings which were printed on everything, capitalized and underlined in red, "if you can read, you could practically *fly* one of these things."

"Well, not quite," said the man seriously, "although I think a fellow who had worked on them could."

"Could you?" I asked, knowing full well that I couldn't, even after 50,000 years on the production line.

He said he thought he could — but he admitted he never had.

While I was amusing myself, Dusty returned and bellowed, *"Bowman!"* through the ship. I left the flight deck and climbed back to the tunnel through the bomb bay. The lights (not very bright ones) were on now in the tunnel, and Dusty was struggling with the fittings and asking loudly why the devil the army didn't take Mac-Gregor.

Fitting a de-icer tube into place after the others were up was not an easy job. (I can practically hear Dusty snort at that masterpiece of understatement.) Sometimes we had to take down most of the tubing we had already installed. Then, while I unscrewed bolts and removed clips, Dusty struggled to loosen ("untighten" was his word) the bulkhead fittings while he cussed Mr. Mac-Gregor with a proficiency gained by twenty-three years in Uncle Sam's navy.

From my position on the stool, I inspected the additions to the tunnel while I worked. In the rear was a big metal box for a camera, which could be swung down over the opening to the hatch to take aerial photographs. All around the sides of the tunnel were little round portable oxygen jugs for the crew to carry when they had to move about the ship. There were also little boxes of electric outlets where they could plug in their electrically heated flying suits. Down under the window-sill there was a dictaphone-like mouthpiece attached to a tube.

"What's that for?" I asked Dusty.

"Er——that's the relief tube," he said euphemistically with an embarrassed, apologetic cough.

"The plumbing!" I thought wisely and made a mental note to tell C.M., for it explained a small hole in the side of the ship which we had often wondered about.

Dusty and I moved from ship to ship down Bomber Row until finally when the one o'clock whistle blew we were working on the first ship inside the door on the production line. Dusty was completely exhausted, but I was quite chipper, all of which proves that there is quite a difference between loosening bulkhead fittings and loosening bolts. (Dusty, in spite of his bad qualities, always took the harder jobs for himself and left the easier ones for me.)

When we got back to Station 20, Mr. MacGregor greeted us cheerfully and stamped the ships we had done off the chart above his bench.

"How did you like working on the field?" he asked with a leer.

"Swell!" I said.

"*Hell!*" said Dusty.

CHAPTER EIGHTEEN

T *HE* mysterious Mr. Tompkinson ducked into the bomb bay one night for a brief chat with Pappy's crew, by which time C.M., who had scarcely seen him since the first night, had decided that her leadman was somebody entirely different. Mr. Tompkinson brought news to the bomb bay of *increased production.* One more ship was to be moved every day, he announced impressively.

"We've got to get things going," said Mr. Tompkinson, rubbing his hands (which were quite clean) together. "Getting things going" was a favorite expression of leadmen and foremen, but just what Mr. Tompkinson meant by it in this particular case C.M. did not find out until the next night when he transferred her and a girl named Irma to another station "in electrical" under a Mr. Snell.

C.M. always referred to this event in a hurt tone of voice as the time Mr. Tompkinson sold her up the river, although I pointed out to her kindly that if he transferred the dumbest girl in his crew (that was Irma) to Mr. Snell he had to make up for it by transferring something extra special like herself as well. She brightened at this and said did I really think so, and I said I did. After all, Irma was living proof that Consolidated will hire practically anybody and fire practically nobody. For three months she had been passed down the list of Station 18 installations by Mr. Tompkinson until right before her transfer she was putting the covers over the lights in the bomb bay, a bolt and nut job which she did laboriously with the wrong size wrench until C.M. pointed out one night that she had the right size one in her tool box.

I said to Mr. Snell, who was my favorite leadman on the line, that it was too bad Mr. Tompkinson had transferred his dummy to him; and Mr. Snell looked bewildered and said, "Which one?" This remark crushed C.M. completely when I carried it back to her, and she cursed Mr. Tompkinson roundly for throwing a pearl like her to the swine at Station 17. I said that after all Mr. Snell couldn't be expected to know which was the dumb one, Irma or her, until he had seen both at work; but C.M. said by golly, he ought to know by *just looking*. She said forlornly that she wished she were back in the bomb bay where people appreciated her. The bomb bay crew, however, had been completely broken up. C.M. was working in the tunnel, Emeline was doing clean-up "around the corner" in the paint, and Pappy was handling some complex wiring which the electricians referred to as "putting in the noses."

I tried to cheer C.M. by telling her how much happier she would be under Mr. Snell than Mr. Tompkinson, who obviously had *no* sense of loyalty if he would simply cast her off after her five weeks of hard and faithful service. Mr. Snell was a week-old leadman, so new that he didn't have "Leadman" printed down the side of his button yet and people still said, "Is *he* a leadman?" I knew his appointment had been popular with his crew, for I had heard the girls of Station 17, which was a regular hen-roost, discussing the matter when the vacancy occurred. They had said in effect that if Snell were not made leadman, virtue was obviously its own and *only* reward. Blondie, who was seven years out of Texas but still pronounced Snell as Snay-ul, told me that Snay-ul was the hardest, fastest worker on the line. He was a little fellow, so short that C.M. was surprised to find even herself on a level with a man's eyes; and he walked very straight and belligerently

146

with his arms at his sides, elbows bent out as if he expected someone to hit him. Since he revised his life story every time he told it to me, I never found out if he really had been a prize fighter; but his ears, which gave his face a cheerful brown mug look, were definitely cauliflower. Mr. Snell had round blue eyes and a straight, wide smile; in fact, everything about him had the clicking efficiency of a mechanical toy. I always told C.M. that I would like to have a copy of Mr. Snell that I could take home and wind up to amuse me; but since this was not possible, I went out of my way to engage him in long and involved conversations so that I could watch him. He was the only person on the line who never looked sleepy or bored; and whenever he bustled up into a ship to check the wiring his girls had been doing, it was (tritely but truly) as if a fresh breeze had blown in.

C.M. had to admit that Mr. Snell was an improvement over Mr. Tompkinson, especially after I showed her his fine trap-like smile; and she even looked more kindly on the tunnel, which was her new place of work, once she had learned how to get in and out of it. The entrance to the tunnel was a step-like five rung ladder which was hooked over the edge of the hatch. This ladder was practically vertical, and the distance from the last rung to the floor was surprisingly one and a half times the distance between the other rungs. To add to these difficulties, a person had to ascend and descend with a tool box and a light in one hand and a stool and a motor in the other. Ascending was really easier than descending, if there were any choice, although, as C.M. said sourly the first time she tried it, you had to *climb* in but you could always *fall* out. Most new-comers, preparing to descend for the first time, inspected the ladder timidly and carefully from the top and then, drawing back a step, asked some old-timer like me, "Is it better to go down frontwards or backwards?" C.M. (and

I was proud of her!) mastered her entrances and exits quickly, unlike Irma, who the last time I saw her was still making a trip up or down for each separate piece of equipment, tool box, light, stool, and motor. This made C.M. feel superior, and she was her old self again.

She mastered her entrances . . . quickly.

C.M. was impressed by the confusion inside and the excitement outside the tunnel, but she insisted loyally that the main advantage working in the tunnel had over working in the bomb bay was just that: she was working *over* the bomb bay. *She* got to drop things for a change, instead of having them dropped on her. This was dangerously true. In her new job, which was wiring the three little blue lights along the top of the tail, she had to straddle the entrance to the tunnel, one foot on the top of the door and one foot on the hand railing which ran along the side.

Then *everybody* who climbed in or out of the tunnel had to duck between her legs. When C.M. was in this position, I, believing that discretion was the better part of valor, entered the tunnel through the bomb bay by the "back door."

The ship in which C.M. and Mr. Snell's other girls were working was always a cozy place. Everybody called everybody else "Honey," modified every noun with "li'l old," and buzzed madly over the latest gossip of the line.

Blondie and Phyllis were the old timers of the group. They were absolutely the cleanest girls on the line, and they amazed us, even before we got to know them, because they could arrive for work in spotless, creased slacks and leave work at one o'clock with their slacks still spotless and still creased. *They* could wear pink or baby blue or beige slacks and keep them clean. *They* could wear sheer blouses with long, full sleeves and *they* could wear shoes which were so white that their owners were perturbed when someone accidentally stepped on them. *They* could keep their hair in intricate coiffures—up in beautiful curls one day and down in beautiful curls the next, with the whole thing topped by fresh or artificial flowers carefully chosen to match the costume jewelry they were wearing for the day.

We in our striped T-shirts and dusty blue slacks did not see how they did it. We asked Babe of the bomb bay how some girls managed to keep so clean, and she replied, snippily, that some girls had clean jobs and other girls made it their job to keep clean. Since C.M., with the dust and dural in her hair and on the seat of her pants, was doing the same type of work that Blondie and Phyllis were, we decided that, in Babe's opinion anyway, Blondie and Phyllis fell into the second classification. *It was true* that they carried towels around with them to wipe their hands on and newspapers to sit on—and *not once* this summer did

C.M. or I go into the restroom that they were not there, combing their hair or washing their hands; but they did do their jobs with effortless smoothness, the clean way and the easy way, while C.M. and I in our inexperience worked the hard and dirty way.

Blondie and Phyllis, who seemed about our age, amazed us by talking about their "little old kids," a 10-year-old daughter and an 11-year-old son respectively. They compared their problems of child care with Verna, a quiet redhaired girl, who also had a young son and daughter. Blondie's daughter was in Texas with her grandmother for the summer, and Phyllis's son stayed at night with a neighbor while Phyllis worked. Verna, whose husband worked over on the Coronado line, had what we thought was the most sensible solution to the problem. She paid her sister a salary to act as housekeeper for her family. After all, Verna said wisely, the job at home was just as much a job as the one on the production line and the person who held it should be paid accordingly.

Martha, the daughter of an army major and the newest member of the crew, was married to a riveter farther down the line. (Marriage, she said, was "interesting.") She was a pale, thin girl with a mass of dark hair. She told C.M. that she was not supposed to work hard because she had a heart murmur—and she didn't. In fact, after only a week on the job, she loafed like a professional, making a job that she could do in half a night last all night. Most of the girls in electrical took full-time for a half-time job. The other half of the time they devoted to the gossip of the line.

The choicest bit of gossip at the time C.M. was transferred to the tunnel was the bitter battle being waged by two girls in electrical for the affection of a sour lad named Jeff. Lena was 43 ("With a husband and a son in the navy," someone contributed juicily.) and Sally was 21, the same age as Jeff. Lena always dashed out of the ship when the whistle blew, intercepted Jeff on his way to meet Sally, upbraided him bitterly during the smoke periods, and then came back to the ship to tell Sally that she would "beat up on her" if she didn't stay away from Jeff. Sally, in turn, recounted her troubles to the girls in electrical, tried to avoid the ship in which Lena was working — and kept on seeing Jeff.

C.M. recounted these details with relish to me, since I was working down "around the corner" where I missed all the gossip.

All week the line buzzed with what Jeff had said to Lena in the ship at Station 17 and what Lena had said to Sally at the fountain and what Sally had said, until at last it all melted into "Sally said——," "Lena said——," and "Jeff said——." The three of them were pointed out to those who didn't know them by those who did: Jeff, pale and glum; Sally, small and shaggy; Lena, lined and haggard — with blue velvet bows in her hair.

Saturday night *it happened*, as everybody on the line had said wisely it would. When we came up to Station 20 after lunch (I had coaxed C.M. into eating "around the corner" with me, a fact which she will always hold against me.), everybody said had we seen *it* and we said had we seen *what*.

"*The fight!* Sally and Lena fought over Jeff."

By the end of the evening we had received a blow-by-blow account of the whole affair, for everybody on the line (except us, C.M. pointed out bitterly) seemed to have been an eye-witness to at least one small thing himself.

"Sally really tore that other lady apart!" marvelled the blank-faced school-teacher from Arkansas who put up the waterproof pockets for the signal flares. "Why, she had chunks of her hair in *both* hands!" (The school-teacher from Arkansas was the one who had told me loftily that *she* had made a perfect grade on her I.Q. test — 100 !)

"You bet! Sally didn't start it, but she really finished it," the woman who hung the straps for the oxygen bottles agreed with satisfaction. She was the mother of the boy who worked with Jeff on the belly turrets, and she strongly disapproved of a woman practically *her* age running after a boy "Sonny's" age.

"*Mais oui !*" chirped the toothless old man who installed the tiny doors that led into the bomb bay from the tunnel, and always embellished his conversation with French phrases that combined a labored high school accent with a slow southwestern drawl. "Lena's blouse was practically ripped off when they took her up to Billings' office after lunch. *Mon dieu !*"

"They'll fire both of the girls, I bet," prophesied the friendly Texan who presided over our tool crib. She had favored Sally in the fight because Sally was a Texan too, and the woman at the tool crib felt that all Texans should stick together against "them Californians," who did not appreciate the generosity of the Texans in dropping what they were doing to come to the coast and win the war. (The highest praise we received this summer was when she said, "You girls are nice enough to be Texans !")

"I'd pay good money to see the fight outside," said the little one-armed man from the salvage department, who shook bolts and nuts out of the dust as if he were panning gold.

"Well," said the boy who drove the orange truck up and down the center aisle, "there's one thing 192 has that the other departments don't have — a man the girls will fight over !"

There was no fight outside — for the policemen who escorted the two girls to the gate (they were *both* fired, in line with company policy), sent Sally home first and Lena one hour later. Everybody said that Sally would be re-hired, since she had not started the fight, and Mr. Snell said he certainly hoped so, for Sally was a good worker. The girls in electrical said they could hardly wait to hear all about it from Sally herself.

Sally was re-hired a week later, but by that time the girls were buzzing over something else. In the week that had passed since The Fight, two new girls had been added to the crew at Section 17, the boy who hung the belly turrets with Jeff had been stabbed in a dance hall fight, a clerk had been fired after she had torn up all the office records, and new nose turrets had been added to the ships on the line so that the front looked even more like the back. The night Sally returned a ship had burned down at the corner, and the line moved at 6:30 "smokin" to fill in the hole. The girls "in electrical" buzzed over these more recent happenings and greeted Sally, whose return they had so eagerly looked forward to, with a careless, "Hello, Honey, you back again?"

CHAPTER NINETEEN

ONE night Lindy and I were stringing cables along the wings with Ada, an older woman of 55 who was new on the line. Mr. MacGregor had told us to help her out when we finished our own work. Lindy and I were having a fine time, enjoying the view from the platform and singing "The Eyes of Texas Are Upon You," Lindy's favorite song, which she was swinging bodily as well as vocally. As we started over on the chorus, I spotted Mr. Billings and his red button below at Station 18 and joined in with a warning variation, "The eyes of Billings are upon you, you cannot get away. The eyes of Billings are upon you, all the live long day." Lindy got the idea and dropped her singing to a hum while she busied herself with the cables. We both kept a wary eye on Mr. Billings, Lindy's being more wary than mine because I was terminating in a week anyway. We watched him climb up the ladder into the tunnel of the ship on which we were working and stand there for five minutes, only his legs visible. From the platform, we could see the girls in the tunnel stop their work and gather around the hatch.

"Something's up," said Lindy. "Something's up."

By this time even Ada had stopped work to watch Mr. Billings, who finally climbed down the ladder and stood below at Station 18 reading something from a mimeographed sheet in his hand to the two women who were working at the bench.

"Whatever it is," said Lindy, "they don't like it."

154

Then Mr. Billings, the paper still in his hand, came up the steps to the platform where we three were working.

"Lordy, what have we done now?" murmured Lindy, wiping her hands nervously on the seat of her pants.

Mr. Billings smiled cheerfully; although he didn't lick his chops, it was that kind of a smile. He said he had a little love letter for us. We smiled, the way C.M. and I smile at the principal's jokes in faculty meeting; and Mr. Billings began to read from the mimeographed sheet, reading very fast and skipping sections. Down below I could see Mr. MacGregor looking up worriedly. Mr. Billings was reading something about "state law" and "women in the factory," "hair coverings" and "caps."

"Does that mean we have to wear *caps*?" Lindy asked as he stopped reading.

Mr. Billings said yes, that was what it meant. He seemed pleased that Lindy had caught on so quickly.

"Caps," said Lindy disgustedly.

"Can't we wear turbans or bandanas or nets?" Ada asked.

"No," said Mr. Billings definitely, referring to the sheet in his hand. "Just caps." He seemed to be enjoying himself, and I remembered how on our first night he had told C.M. and me that the company was going to *insist* on girls' wearing hair coverings.

"What kind of caps?" I asked Mr. Billings. He replied graciously that *any* cap was all right—as long as it had a bill on it and covered *all the hair*.

"All?" said Lindy, who had long, curly, reddish-brown hair.

"*All*," said Mr. Billings.

We could not help thinking how our faces would look in caps that covered *all* the hair. It was a depressing thought.

"Why," said Mr. Billings, trying to cheer us, "I just saw

a little girl who looked *so cute* in her cap that I was tempted to ask her for a date!'"

We did not look impressed.

"I'm afraid caps will look rather silly on an older woman like me," said Ada, whose hair was a pleasant salt and pepper grey.

"Oh, *no!*" said Mr. Billings, equal to anything. "I just saw a woman *much older* than you who looked *very attractive* in her cap."

After Mr. Billings had climbed down the steps and up the ladder into the next ship and Mr. MacGregor had called up worriedly, "What's the matter?," we delivered to each other our carefully considered opinion of foremen in general and the foreman of Department 192, in particular — although I pointed out charitably to Lindy that it was a general order for the whole plant, not just for Department 192.

"Even if Billings didn't think it up, he thinks it's a good idea," said Lindy sourly. "Why the boys won't even *look* at us now — and that's just what *he* wants."

By one o'clock, when C.M. and I scrubbed up at the fountain by the time clock, all the girls were recounting with many "he said's" and "I said's" what they had said to Mr. Billings and what Mr. Billings had said to them.

"I just asked Billings how many caps Consolidated had that they wanted to get rid of," announced Phyllis, whom we could not imagine in a work cap since she never wore work clothes. "And he said that nobody had to wear a Consolidated cap — just any little old cap that covered *all* the hair would do."

"I told Billings that if he is going to send home all the girls who come without caps Monday, he'll have to send me home first. I am *not* going to wear a cap," stated Irene, whose hair was piled high in a huge peroxide pompadour.

"Listen, this is the pay-off," said Miller, a mannish-looking woman with a boyish bob who worked "in electrical." "I asked Billings why I have to wear a cap when my hair is *shorter* than his, and he said that even if I shaved it all off, I'd have to wear a cap. 'The order applies to all women workers in the factory,'" she sneered, imitating Mr. Billings.

The women who had worked for more than a year on the line said philosophically that they would get out the ones they had bought last year when everybody was ordered to wear caps that covered *all* the hair.

"It lasted only a couple of weeks," they told C.M. and me comfortingly ; but since C.M. and I were terminating in a week, we were not comforted.

"It'll never work," said C.M., who like me had learned something about the difficulties of keeping girls *in uniform* during four years at San Diego High School. "The foremen don't know how to handle women. They have about as much discipline as a first year teacher. They make rules that they could enforce, but they don't enforce them. Then they make stricter rules that they can't possibly enforce and try to enforce them. I'll bet you a piece of pie and a cup of coffee that they will *never* be able to make every girl in this building or any other building wear a cap that will cover *all* her hair. I bet they can't even do it on Monday. I bet you !"

The rules they could have enforced, according to C.M., were the regulations for women's factory dress which all new employees were given during their Employment Induction. These regulations provided for a uniform slack suit, some type of hair covering if the girl were working near machinery, and sensible low-heeled shoes with closed toes. C.M. and I, like most new employees, I imagine, had accepted these regulations as de rigueur, purchased the prescribed uniforms, hair coverings and shoes, and turned up at work only to find that being "in uniform" marked us as *new* to aircraft work.

The girls we saw wore every type of slacks, from flimsy ones that would have been more appropriate in the boudoir to dungarees, men's pants, and riding breeches. For blouses, they wore crêpe torso affairs that looked as if they had survived the afternoon skirts that originally went with them, sheer long-sleeved numbers with ruffles, peasant things with gay embroidery, striped T-shirts, and, of course, sweaters, especially a popular number sold by the most garish store in town and ribbed through the midriff for the best "sweater girl" effect.

The only really effective hair coverings were worn by the girls who came to work with their hair in curlers. All other coverings were such in name only, definitely enhancing to woman's crowning glory, which was usually swooped up on top of the head in a complex arrangement of combs, curls and flowers (the flowers being considered the hair coverings, we assumed), or spread out in its full length and beauty under the doubtful protection of a colorful chiffon square with two ends tied underneath the hair and the other two above.

Most of the girls did observe the regulation about shoes because it seemed stupid not to. If a girl wanted to dress inappropriately and impractically and spend all her time washing and ironing, that was her choice; and if she wanted to "cover" her hair in such a way that the covering was no protection from dirt, electrical attraction, or motors because she thought she was better looking that way (and certainly she was), that also was her privilege; and any woman could understand why with a choice between beauty and safety, she would take beauty. But nobody could understand why a woman would insist on wearing flat-soled open-toe and open-heel huaraches that skid on steep steps and slippery surfaces and offered no

158

protection against toe-stubbing edges, heavy falling things, or the feet of other people — when they did *nothing* at all for the looks of her feet anyway! Very few people wore regulation slacks or hair coverings, but everybody wore regulation shoes — except Babe of the bomb bay, who padded along on flat sandals and said hello or made a face when a foreman came by so that he wouldn't look at her feet.

But Monday *every* woman in the factory was to wear a regulation hair covering, a cap that covered *all* her hair. Monday every woman without such a covering was to be sent home at the gate, according to the foremen. Monday was going to be *different*.

Monday morning when C.M. and I went downtown to purchase our caps, there was a crowd of unhappy girls, Blondie among them, at the counter, which was piled high with caps — with bills! Blondie said that this was the only store in town that still had caps. They were in two shades of blue — one that matched the regulation uniform and another of faded blue denim.

"They're all the same size, Honey," Blondie told me dispiritedly.

"No," said the sales girl technically, "on some of them the elastic varies as much as a quarter of an inch in back."

Carefully comparing the caps for size, C.M. picked out the smallest she could find and I took the largest. This amounted to a difference of about an eighth of an inch. C.M. put hers on carefully and looked at herself in the mirror.

"Don't you have any more becoming styles?" she asked feebly, after looking at the apparition in the mirror.

The salesgirl swung her gum to the other cheek, jerked her girdle down, and said sympathetically, "Well, with your face, Kid, what can you expect?"

Abashed, C.M. said she would take the cap. With

C.M.'s appearance as an example, I charged mine without even trying it on.

"It's only for a week anyway," I told Blondie.

"Why, Honey, is Billings making you buy a cap for just one little old week?"

C.M. and I were quite noble about it.

She looked at the apparition in the mirror.

"If *everybody* is going to have to wear a cap, then we will wear caps too," we said.

At home I tried my cap on, skinning my hair up under it. I must say it didn't do much for me except to make my face look squarer and my glasses rounder. What C.M.'s did to her, I shall not mention.

In our caps and our big safety glasses, we felt completely disguised so that we were surprised when the bus driver recognized us.

"What are you wearing those things for?" she asked as we showed her our passes.

We explained about the new order and the caps that had to cover *all* the hair.

"Huh," she said, shifting gears, "that'll be harder to enforce than prohibition."

It was too. The only difference was that when they couldn't enforce prohibition, they repealed it.

When we got off the bus at Gate Two, we looked curiously at the other girls, who were looking more curiously at us because we were the only ones wearing caps that covered *all* our hair. Most of the girls looked the way they usually did. Some of them had on hair coverings, snoods, bandanas, nets and turbans, and some of them didn't. Nobody had on a cap. We had been told that the girls would be stopped at the gate if they weren't wearing caps, but nobody stopped them. C.M. and I decided that the girls were probably waiting until they got into the building to put on their caps. Inside the building a few were wearing caps, but these were perched at a rakish angle on the back of their curls. Then C.M. and I decided that the rest of them were probably waiting until the whistle blew at 4:30 to put on their caps. We wished we had waited until then. We felt rather silly, and the backs of our necks were cold.

The 4:30 whistle blew, and only a few more caps went on. The girls with their caps set on top of their hair went to work. The girls with turbans and bandanas and snoods on their hair went to work. So did the girls who had *nothing* on their hair. At 4:35 Mr. Billings started down the line, systematically looking into every ship, ferreting out the ones without hair coverings, giving them little slips, and sending them home. He made the girls wearing hair coverings other than caps cover *all* their hair, but he didn't send them home. Lindy he told to tie her hair up in a scarf, and he waited until she did it.

"Uh-uh, no horns," said Mr. Billings, and he waited until she tucked her bangs in.

All night the excitement raged. Mr. Billings carried his little slips around in his pocket and went dashing off after any girl he spotted without a hair covering. Some of the girls went home peaceably, and some refused point blank.

"You'll have to fire me," said one girl, "because I won't go and I won't quit."

Mr. Billings backed down at that and told her to wrap her head in a towel for that night.

The girls stopped work to discuss the latest developments. The leadmen said they wanted to know how they could get their ships out if the foreman was going to send all the girls home. The timekeepers climbed into the ships to identify the girls in their departments because they all looked different with their hair covered. The men had a fine time laughing at the girls.

Two girls worked all night in bright sporty caps with little signs pinned on them: "Don't laugh, fellows! You'll be next." One old woman came up to me, cackling happily. "Them foremens think the men will stop looking at the girls if they have to wear caps, but men have looked at me tonight who never looked at me before!" She winked wickedly as she went off down the line. The assistant foreman announced that he had an eye for a pretty girl just like any other man, but he had a lot more respect for a girl who looked as if she had come on the job prepared to work. At this, the girls snorted, "Huh!"

During eleven o'clock "smokin" the girls across the line in Department 194 started to circulate a petition asking that the order be relaxed to allow turbans and bandanas as well as caps.

"My god!" said one of the foremen. "We've tried all year to get them to wear turbans and bandanas, and now they're *asking* to wear them!"

The deadline for wearing caps was pushed back to Wednesday so that they would be available at the store in the plant. Until then every girl was to wear a turban or bandana that *completely* covered the hair. On Tuesday the girls who had been sent home Monday night came back. The clerks in the foremen's offices, who had been sent home too, appeared wearing enormous fuzzy knitted turbans.

"What do they think we'll catch our hair in—pencil sharpeners?" they scoffed.

By the time that Wednesday came, it was obvious that Mr. Billings and the other foremen had been vanquished. It was impossible (1) to get the girls in caps, (2) to keep them in caps, (3) to make them put their hair under the caps—unless the foremen were willing to devote all of their time to achieve these three things. On Wednesday Lindy was wearing a regulation cap, but her "horns" and her "mane" were out again. Irene was wearing a bandana, but her magnificent blond pompadour was uncovered. Miller had set a boy's beanie on the back of her boyish bob. Blondie had taken the bill off her regulation cap and was wearing the rest of it on the back of her head like a tam. Phyllis, who was now wearing her hair down over her shoulders in a mass of tiny curls, added the final touch to the farce with a triangular felt peasant cap that had a gay bunch of felt flowers attached to each side. The *only* woman wearing a cap that covered *all* her hair was the Women's Counselor, who was trying to be an *example*.

CHAPTER TWENTY

W*HENEVER* we were tired and dirty and bored this summer (and *sometimes* we were,) C.M. and I used to cheer ourselves by planning dramatic ways in which we could announce to Mr. Billings that we were terminating our employment at Consolidated. We detailed these plans to our fellow workers, who agreed enviously that if we were going to have the pleasure of terminating we should do it in style. Our best and most dramatic scheme, we all thought — although we never did work out the mechanical details — was to walk up to Mr. Billings, announce with dignity, "We terminate!" and pull a string so that our dusty blue uniforms would fall off and we would appear before him resplendent in our beautiful summer suits which we had worn only twice all summer because of the cursed Swing Shift.

What really happened was very undramatic. We simply gave our three days' notice to Mr. Billings, who wrote our names down in his little notebook under "Tuesday" and sent us over to the Personnel Office for a pre-termination interview.

"Just a formality," he said, since we had been hired with the understanding that it was only for summer vacation.

The Pre-termination Clerk gave us a form so that we could get an Availability Certificate if we ever wanted one.

"It was awfully nice of you to come down and help out," she said sociably, and we felt as if we had been canning peaches instead of building bombers.

She sent us back to Mr. Ely with a sealed envelope that evidently contained our official termination papers. Mr. Ely smiled when we gave it to him. He smiled and said that we had been good and conscientious workers. Then he smiled and said that Consolidated and he personally appreciated what we had done. We smiled. Mr. Ely smiled. Feeling quite important, we went off to announce to Mr. Snell and Mr. MacGregor that we were terminating on Tuesday. Since they had not been told that we were merely temporary workers, Mr. Snell said, "Oh!" and Mr. MacGregor said, "Oh my god!" (I am *sure* that is what he said, but C.M. insists that it was "Oh thank god!" and the expression I interpreted as consternation was merely relief. I think she is still just a little miffed that Mr. Snell didn't say "Oh my god!" when he found out that he was going to lose *her*.)

Monday night Mr. Billings came down the line with two new girls, one of whom he delegated to Mr. Snell to take C.M.'s place and one to Mr. MacGregor to take mine. Mr. Snell and Mr. MacGregor deposited them in our care with instructions that we were to teach them our jobs. The girls looked bewildered and confused and impressed and reminded us how bewildered and confused and impressed we had been on our first night two months before. Having them come in to fill our places made us realize that we had really been doing something to "help" during the summer. We hadn't been merely "extra." Our jobs were not going to be absorbed by other people in addition to their regular work. We had to be replaced, woman for woman, job for job.

Tuesday was our last night—the last night we would wear our big green buttons, the last night we would open our lunch boxes for the inspection of the guards, the last night we would punch the time clock, the last night we would study the chart above the bench, the last night we would climb in and out of the ships, the last night we would watch the line move. The last night!

"Your last night!" everybody said enviously when we came up to the bench.

Some asked, "Are you sorry to go?" and others, "Are you glad?," depending on how they liked working on the production line themselves. Mary, who thought it was fun, said, "Are you sorry?"; and Dusty, who thought he needed a vacation (I don't know why), said "Are you glad?" We explained that we were sorry we were going tonight, but that we were glad we weren't coming back tomorrow. We realized that when we left the plant that night at one o'clock, we would never be able to enter it again. As far as we were concerned, the world of Building Four in which we had lived all summer would no longer exist. We felt as if we were closing a book which we had been reading for so long that the world in it had become real to us. When we closed the book, that world would no longer exist for us, except in the book. It was this sense of complete finality that made us treasure every minute of the last night.

At eleven o'clock our termination procedure was to begin, and when the whistle blew for "smokin" we realized that we were finishing our last ship.

"Come on, Kids," said Dusty, ducking down the hatch. *"You're through!* Somebody else will finish this one."

"Not on your life," we told him. "We're not going to leave our last ship unfinished."

C.M. put up her last clip and I tightened my last bulkhead fitting, *really tight* for Mr. MacGregor. We climbed down out of the ship and looked up at the number chalked on the tail. It was a much larger number than the one that had been on the ship in front of Station 20 our first night. A great many Liberators had gone around the line while we had been there.

Mr. Ely had told us to start our termination procedure at eleven o'clock so that we would be sure to complete it by one. All we had to do was to go down the length of the line and collect a clearance slip from each tool crib along the way. Then we were to check out at Mr. Ely's office

It was the last night we would punch in at the clock.

and at Personnel. Mr. Ely had said he didn't think that would take nearly two hours, but, of course, he didn't know us very well.

We seemed to have tools checked out at every tool crib

on the line. I kept expecting somebody to demand one which we had lost, but nobody did. In fact, after we had collected all our clearance slips, we still had a stringer wrench, a pair of glasses, two drills, and half a dozen chuck keys that nobody had asked for. We presented these to the man at the last tool crib, who was a little worried about how he should account for them on his records.

The last tool crib was at the very end of the building between the first station on the right and the last station on the left. Standing there on our last night between the ship that was finished and the ship that was just begun, we felt the greatest thrill of real accomplishment that we had had all summer. The finished ship at the end of the line was a night shift ship, one that we had worked on, and it once had been like the ship now at the first of the line, just three great sections, tail with bare insides, stubby wings without spreading tips, empty nose, all held together by a great skeletal jig.

"You know, we really did do something this summer," said C.M.

"Don't I know we did!" I said, looking at the ships and then at my hands, with the callouses on the palms and the cuts on the knuckles and not one fingernail that extended beyond the tip of the finger.

On our way back to Station 20 we said goodbye to everyone along the way. It seemed very important that we say goodbye to all the people we knew because we realized that once we left Building Four we would never see them again. We were especially fond of them, I think, because in a sense they belonged to us. They were characters in the book that we were writing, and we knew them much better than they would ever know us.

When we got back to Station 20, the midnight whistle was shrieking above the sounds of the line. As C.M. bustled off on some mysteriously complex errand that involved trading her tools with one of the girls "in electrical," I said goodbye to Mr. MacGregor. During the summer I had grown rather fond of the old slave driver, and I could honestly say (as I did) that I had enjoyed working under him. In reply he delivered what was probably his usual farewell speech.

"Bowman," he said, shaking my hand and looking me straight in the eye. "I want you to know that you have been *above average* for a lady worker."

Before I could murmur my thank you for these kind words, Mr. Carter came up with C.M. in tow.

"Get these girls out of here," he said to Mr. MacGregor, as if we weren't there. "They were supposed to be at Personnel an hour ago."

Mr. MacGregor passed the message on to us while Mr. Carter went striding off down the line at the greatest speed we had ever seen a Red Button go.

"You were supposed to be at Personnel an hour ago," he said sternly.

"Yes, sir," we said. "Goodbye!"

We staggered up to Mr. Ely's office. The secretary (the new one) pounced on us and said we were supposed to be at Personnel an hour ago. The phone rang and it was Personnel saying that we were supposed to be there an hour ago. Mr. Billings and Mr. Ely got up and said we were supposed to be at Personnel an hour ago. The secretary grabbed each of us by the hand while somebody gave her directions for finding Personnel. In the excitement we tried to tell Mr. Billings and Mr. Ely how nice everyone had been, how much we had learned — and what fun we had had. We wanted them to know that building bombers had been a memorable experience. Mr. Billings looked pleased and said we should tell the Personnel Director how we felt. He'd be glad to hear about it, Mr. Billings thought. Mr. Ely patted us kindly on the shoulder (gently guiding us toward the exit) and said we should build bombers again *next* summer. Everybody said, "Goodbye — and good luck!" and somebody said, "They were supposed to be at Personnel an hour ago."

A delegation of three was waiting for us when we *finally* arrived at Personnel. A big man (who *glowered* at us) counted our tools, which we had packed in our lunch boxes with all our other possessions, scornfully listed them on a pink "Permit to Remove Personal Property from the Plant," and viciously taped our lunch boxes so tight that when we went to pay our bus fare on the way home, it took a knife to open them. A little man (who *ignored* us) handed over our last pay-checks without interrupting his telephone conversation. And a woman who acted as if she had taken her job as a personal favor to the president of the company himself, daintily extracted our termination papers from our soiled fingers. We apologized to the three of them for our tardiness; but the big man continued to glower at us, the little man continued to ignore us — and the woman said sweetly, *Oh so sweetly*, "That's *perfectly* all right!"

We promptly eliminated the three of them from the all-embracing love for Consolidated with which we had left Building Four. But we were determined to tell *somebody* how much we had enjoyed our summer on the production line.

"I wonder if we could speak to the Personnel Director," said C.M. The woman raised one eyebrow ever so slightly. "We're teachers," C.M. plunged on, as the eyebrow went higher, "and we'd like to tell somebody how successful, for the teachers at least, the program of summer work has been." The woman gracefully lowered the eyebrow and raised it again. "We feel," continued C.M., fixing a fascinating stare on the eyebrow, "I mean it seems to us . . . We think . . ."

Somewhat incoherently, her earnest tribute trickled to a stop.

The woman looked at her disdainfully, raised *both* her neatly plucked eyebrows, and lowered her carefully shadowed lids.

"Why don't you write a letter about it?" she said, speaking with the careful sweetness of hydrochloric acid dripping over lump sugar. The end of one eyebrow quivered wearily.

"Thank you. We shall," I said quickly—and with *remarkable* self-restraint, I thought. I could see C.M. coming to a boil.

"That frozen-faced, syrup-voiced lump of sugared venom!" she sputtered as we went outside. "I hate her. I won't work in the same airplane factory with her. I won't build bombers within ten miles of her. I'll terminate! I'll resign! I'll quit!"

"You've already quit," I reminded her soothingly as we handed our termination papers to the guard at the gate.

The guard stood aside for us to pass. We half turned to look back at Building Four—and then we went through the gate. We were on the *outside* again.

While we waited at the bus stop, we watched the guards prepare for the crowds that would be coming out when the whistle blew at one o'clock. Across the plant we could see through the open door of Building Four, but to us the scene had the flat two-dimensional look of a picture thrown on a screen. Every detail was completely familiar, yet completely unreal. Already we could not believe that the production line still existed—that tomorrow and all the other tomorrows, the three big sections of the B-24's would be brought down from the Parts Plant, that they would be riveted together at the beginning of the line, that they would be moved past Station 20 and around the corner, out the door and down Bomber Row — and that at last they would actually fly !

We had helped to build bombers, but there were many more bombers to be built.

CHAPTER TWENTY-ONE

T HE dollars that we made this summer were not many. We added them up the night before we quit and C.M. said, looking glumly at the total, that anybody who thought we had been motivated by anything but patriotism in its purest form could just look at our pay-checks after the government got through with them. Just look at them, she said ; and I admitted that financially the most successful thing about our summer was that we didn't have time to spend the money that we didn't make, so at least we were not in debt.

But if the dollars that we made were few, the bombers that we built were many. We added them up too on the last night, and C.M. looked proudly at the sum and said she'd just like to see what that many Liberators could do to Berlin.

The last night we told everyone on the line how many bombers we had built during the summer (for we always referred to our own small contribution in turning out a Liberator as *building* a bomber). We even told Mr. Ely, who looked very impressed, although I have an idea that he was more impressed by the fact that we had counted them than by the fact that we had built them. I suppose the number was infinitesimal in comparison to the production figures of the aircraft industry ; but it was terrifically impressive to us that there were that many Liberators, *that many* which we had helped to put into the air. When we looked up and saw one, dark and powerful like a great thunderbird — and yet completely familiar to us — we had a very strange feeling in the corners of our stomachs, because that particular Liberator might be one of ours.

Every time we saw the word "Liberator" in a headline or the great flying shape in the newsreel, we were amazed that anything so newsworthy could have such a personal meaning to us. We knew that it was Liberators which were leading the invasion into France and bombing the great industrial cities of Germany, but to us a Liberator was a place in which we had worked night after night. Its color, its shape, its walls were completely familiar to us. We had clipped tubes in the nose where the bombardier looked through his secret bombsight down on the target, we had sat in the seat where the pilot guided his ship over enemy territory, we had worked in the bomb bay from which those great bombs dropped. We had seen Liberators when they were only great sections held together by a jig; we had watched them go around the line, becoming more and more like airplanes; and we had stood under their great spreading wings, knowing that at last they would actually fly.

We knew that a Liberator was built by many people and many hours; and whenever in a newsreel we saw the inside of the tunnel with the oxygen bottles strapped into place, the belly turret hung down in its hole, the electric wires strung neat and firm along the sides, we saw Joe throwing the bottles up into the ship and whistling "As Time Goes By;" we saw Jeff swearing ostentatiously and carefully lowering the ball turret into place; we saw Blondie and Phyllis, crisp and clean, stringing the wires and talking about their children. After a summer on the production line we looked at a Liberator the way you gaze in awe at a great tapestry when the note under it says that it took a hundred women twenty years to make it.

Liberators are just that hand-made. They are made by

all sorts of people ; people who loaf on the job and people who work so hard and fast that you know they feel a life depends on them, people who do their jobs poorly and awkwardly and people who do them with the smooth speed of masters. They are made by people like Pappy and Emeline and Dusty and Mary and Sparky. A few of them were made this summer by us.

That's why when a big four-motored, double-ruddered airplane flies overhead now, we don't have to wait for anybody before we say it :

"That's a Liberator !"

Maybe it's one we helped to build.

"That's a Liberator!"

EPILOGUE (1999)
CONSTANCE BOWMAN REID

The day at the end of the summer of 1943 when C.M. and I "terminated" was not by any means the end of the story. We went back to teaching in our classrooms at San Diego High School, but there were illustrations still to be finished and drafts of chapters to be worked into a unified whole. I remember that I did not get around to learning the names of my students until Halloween.

Also, of course, there was the problem of finding a publisher. The only person we knew with even a remote connection to publishing was Hal Brucker, who represented the firm that printed the high school's yearbook. In January 1944 he took a bound copy of the manuscript and illustrations to the Public Relations Department at Consolidated Vultee. They liked it and turned it over to the editor of their company publication, *Plane Talk,* who passed it on to several publishers. These looked at it, also liked it ("accurate and amusingly presented"), but said that although a year earlier it would have been a natural, it was now "dated."

With what we now hope was remarkable prescience, our friend Hal Brucker objected: "I believe it will be of interest to many, many people for a long time to come."

By February our bound manuscript was in the hands of David Legerman, an editor at Longmans, Green. He thought that our story might help to raise the "sagging morale on the home front." But there was a problem, as the editor of *Plane Talk* reported: "Mr. Legerman naturally wants to satisfy himself that the manuscript, although it came into his hands through the Public Relations Department of Consolidated Vultee, is not a 'fake' concoction that department has cooked up."

The very idea!

C.M. was delegated to convince Mr. Legerman that we were real high school teachers to whom everything really had happened. With her letter to him she enclosed a photo of us in our uniforms and safety glasses—an outfit, as she pointed out, that no woman would wear unless required to do so.

On March 7, 1944, we received a telegram: HAVE DECIDED TO PUBLISH YOUR BOOK.

We learned later that Mr. Legerman and his colleagues had had a great laugh over the unintentional double entendre of our manuscript title, *We Were Available*. As an alternative the sales department suggested *Slacks and Callouses*. C.M. and I had no objection to changing the title. (Nobody—including this English teacher—realized that as a noun the word is spelled *calluses*. This error was pointed out only recently by a former student whose spelling checker rejected *callouses*.) We did object to the line proposed for the dust jacket: "How 2 LADY school teachers solved the MANpower shortage in a bomber plant." Mr. Legerman—who customarily addressed us as "lambs," "dears," or "girls"—wrote that the line, like the title, was going to remain "by popular acclaim."

Toward the end of August 1944 the book was in the bookstores. There were lines out to the sidewalk at our first book signing—I writing appropriately personal words, C.M. doing quick personalized sketches. (She is a marvel at that.) People almost always bought more than one copy, sometimes as many as half a dozen to send to friends and relatives overseas. Copies went so fast that the bookstores were hard put to keep a supply in stock.

C.M. and I made a promotional visit to the B-24 production line and punched a time clock for a newspaper photographer. The *San Diego Union* ran a story on how *Slacks and Calluses* came to Convair in "spic and span tailored suits, high heels, and picture hats." It was our summer's dream come true.

I have always wished that an account of this visit could have been included in the book. We had been concerned about the reaction of our fellow workers for although we had changed the names, the disguises were pretty thin. As it turned out they were delighted to see us, they were pleased to be in a book, and most of all they were proud that their contribution to the war effort was being recognized.

The reaction of our fellow teachers was not always delight in our having done what we had so brashly announced we were going to do. One colleague told me, with a certain amount of pleasure, that the librarian at the city's main library had dismissed the "bestseller" status of *Slacks and Calluses* by remarking that *anyone* could write *one* book.

The possibility of further collaboration had in fact ended. C.M.'s husband, Fred Allen, was in medical school at the University of Nebraska in Omaha, and C.M. had obtained a position in that university's art department. This unfortunately was not in Omaha but in Lincoln, so she and Fred became the first "commuting" married couple I knew. She still recalls how in California driving the distance between the two cities had not seemed like much, but in Nebraska it was "a lot."

During the summer of 1945 I visited C.M. So as to be able to go out and paint "on location," members of the art department regularly pooled gas coupons, gas rationing having continued even after victory in Europe. I was posing for them when we heard on the radio that the United States had dropped a new kind of bomb on a Japanese town called Hiroshima.

Fred finished medical school, interned, did a tour of duty as a flight surgeon with the U.S. Air Force during the Korean war, and ultimately established himself in private practice back in San Diego. During this time C.M. learned a remarkable amount about medicine and wrote some verses about the ills to which the human body is subject. One of these concluded "even the anus can pain us"—a line that Ogden Nash himself would surely have envied.

C.M. and Fred had a son in 1949 and later, when she was between 42 and 45, three daughters—ahead of her time again. Since then her drawing has been limited to PTA and garden club posters along with Christmas cartoons of the family, which now includes seven grandchildren.

After the war I went back for an advanced degree at the University of California in Berkeley. There I met Neil Reid, known as "Dan" to his friends, a returning veteran who had been a pilot in the Army Air Force. (He had not, however, flown B-24s.) We married in 1950 and settled in San Francisco. Dan became a lawyer specializing in aviation litigation. He has continued flying and aviation has always been a very important part of our family life. We have a daughter and a son and, now, three grandchildren and a stepgranddaughter.

After we were married, Dan encouraged me to try writing short stories. I received several kind rejection slips and had one story published in the anthology *Story*. It wasn't long before I realized that fiction was not my metier. I turned to writing magazine articles. *Scientific American* published one of these, an article about my brother-in-law's application of the newly invented computer to a problem in pure mathematics. A publisher read the article and asked if I would write a little book on numbers for him. Encouraged by my sister and my brother-in-law, both distinguished mathematicians, I agreed. The result was *From Zero to Infinity.* This has become something of a classic, having been continuously in print since its publication in 1955. After writing and publishing several other books that explained mathematical ideas in a nontechnical way, I became interested in the lives of mathematicians. I have published five full-length biographies and a number of shorter biographical pieces. How I came to write about mathematics and mathematicians is as unlikely a story as that of *Slacks and Calluses,* but I have recounted it in other places.*

Over the years I became somewhat embarrassed by *Slacks and Calluses.* In those days C.M. and I had a way of writing in capital letters, as we also talked. The publishers wisely changed our capitals to italics, but they would have been wiser yet to have eliminated them altogether. When, a few years ago, Jim Lunbeck, a member of our family, asked me if he could read the book, I cautioned him that I had been very young when I wrote it. But he found it "a lot of fun to read." More important, he thought it was probably unique as a contemporaneously written account of life in a defense factory during World War II. It was he who suggested that we consider republishing it.

In the past, on occasion, I had glanced at the book. Now, in preparation for submitting it to the Smithsonian Institution Press, I reread *Slacks and Calluses* from cover to cover for the first time in more than half a century. It was one of the strangest experiences I have ever had.

It's exactly the way it was.

---

*D. J. Albers and G. L. Alexanderson, *Mathematical People: Profiles and Interviews* (Boston: Birkhauser, 1985), 269–80. Also Constance Reid, "Being Julia Robinson's Sister," *Notices of the American Mathematical Society* 43:12 (Dec. 1996), 1486–92.